Deirdre Brennan
Máighréad Medbh
Nuala Ní Chonchúir

DIVAS!

an anthology of new
irish women's writing

ARLEN
HOUSE

First published by Arlen House in June 2003

Arlen House
PO Box 222
Galway
Ireland

42 Grange Abbey Road
Baldoyle
Dublin 13

ISBN   1–903631–40–8 paperback

arlenhouse@ireland.com
www.arlenhouse.ie

Typesetting: Arlen House
Printed by: ColourBooks, Baldoyle, Dublin 13

L 136,130   €12-00
821
BRE

contents

Eavan Boland's Preface to *The Wall Reader* (Arlen House, 1979) exists as one of the earliest contemporary articulations within Ireland of the on-going debate over the merits, or otherwise, of women-only writing collections, and the concomitant application of the term 'woman writer'. Not surprisingly, perhaps, the debate has incorporated equally pivotal issues about the literary mainstream and margin: does the creation of a space where women's voices exist principally in relation to other women facilitate a source of creativity and celebration away from the 'jealously male-guarded territory of "Irish Literature"' (Smyth 15), or does such a 'custom made pool' (Donovan 5) simply risk the continued isolation or, worse, ghettoisation of women writers who will be encouraged to continue writing for an already converted audience? The longevity of the debate reflects the longevity of the problem of gender imbalance in the Irish literary tradition.

Women-only anthologies, in particular, have played a crucial role in exposing not only the relative invisibility of women within that tradition, but in revealing the range and quality of Irish women's writing: Ruth Hooley's *The Female Line: Northern Irish Women Writers* (1985), the *Midland Review* edited by Nuala Archer (1986), and Ailbhe Smyth's *Wildish Things* (1989), all incorporated samples of Irish women's writing in all genres, and showed that Irish women

had a long and valuable literary history. And it was A. A. Kelly's *Pillars of the House* (1987) which brought the work of Irish women poets, specifically, to the attention of a contemporary reading public, and contributed to our recognising the dominance of men in an Irish poetic tradition, not just as definitive 'writers', but as men writers who depicted women in very particular and limiting ways.

While arguments against women-only collections are seductive in their ostensible gender egalitarianism – 'we're all equal now as writers' – they are only a step away from a more conventional argument that would see value only in a literary text which 'transcends borders, whether local or national, whether of the mind or of the spirit' (A. Norman Jeffares vxiii). The problem is, however, that 'transcendence' of such borders (including those of gender) has for so long equated, in practice, to fixed and defining categories in which 'writer' came to mean 'man', and literary value was judged, not by criteria that are acknowledged as ideologically inflected and at the mercy of cultural and political hegemonies, but which are, instead, presented as absolute. Gender borders, in particular, then, remain important for a number of reasons: because we know that there is no absolute category of 'writer' any more than there can be an absolute category of value; because in terms of publishing opportunities and reviewing practices, the experience of being a woman writer in Ireland today remains different from being a man writer, particularly in terms of poetry publishing; and, perhaps most importantly, the denial of the specifics of production is equally a denial of the often important

material differences at the heart of the experience of being a writer today. An acceptance of the category 'writer' by women – non-border specific – risks our becoming complicit in a process of silencing other women/writers who are not as yet, or ever likely to be, included in that category: in Ireland, those who write in the Irish language, perhaps, or traveller women, or women from the unionist community in Northern Ireland. Despite sharing the unease, then, of those who feel that writing *by* women only is writing *for* women only, Boland's 1979 defence of women-only space on the basis that 'there can only be a contradiction ... if there is any suspicion that the criteria by which talent is fostered are those by which it is judged' (3), remains as relevant as ever.

Certainly, the three poets contained in this volume – Deirdre Brennan, Máighréad Medbh and Nuala Ní Chonchúir – provide no such ground for suspicion. There is only evidence of a woman-centred confidence and celebration devoid of political separatism; a secure and aware Irishness without a hint of parochialism or insularity; and, above all, a body of work that, in its diversity, suggests as much skill and insight as we could ever wish for in a book of poetry by any writer, whether woman or man. That they are three women becomes a mere celebratory backdrop when confronted with their wonderfully astute observations on the human condition and the world around us – sometimes comical, sometimes sad – and since they are so different in topic and style, one from the other, they force us to question the whole notion of the categories that have remained so central to our contemporary literary world.

All three poets in this volume – the first of a new series of anthologies – work in the lyrical tradition, but beyond the most superficial comparisons, any discussion of them within a cohesive genre is impossible: the diversity and range of the poetry suggests that categories like 'women's writing' or 'Irish women's poetry' are virtually meaningless in relation to quality and skill. From Deirdre Brennan's interest in the natural world, and her rich texturing of language, to the echoes of Máighréad Medbh's rap/rock performance poetry, to Nuala Ní Chonchúir's mixture of the exotic and the local, this is poetry of the finest calibre: pure and simple.

Rebecca Pelan

Women's Studies Centre, NUI, Galway

References:

Archer, Nuala, (ed.), *Midland Review* 3 (1986). Special Issue devoted to Irish women writers.
Donovan, Katie. *Irish Women Writers: Marginalised by Whom?* Dublin: Raven Arts, 1988.
Hooley, Ruth, (ed.), *The Female Line: Northern Irish Women Writers*. Belfast: Northern Ireland Women's Rights Movement, 1985.
Jeffares, A Norman. *Commonwealth Literature: Unity and Diversity in a Common Culture*. (ed.) John Press. London: Heinemann, 1965.
Kelly, A. A. *Pillars of the House: An Anthology of Verse by Irish Women from 1690 to the Present*. Dublin: Wolfhound, 1987.
Smyth, Ailbhe. *Wildish Things: An Anthology of New Irish Women's Writing*. Dublin: Attic, 1989.

DIVAS!

Beneath Castles of White Sail

DEIRDRE BRENNAN

why

As a child I loved reading. My love affair with
poetry started in primary school when our teacher
read Shelley's 'Ode to a Skylark' for the class. I
delighted in the music and rhythm of it, the words
mesmorised me, they were like a heady abandoned
magic potion compared to prose. I was so smitten
that I dashed home to try the new language, locked
myself in the bathroom and wrote 'Ode to a
Butterfly'. My mother, a practical Northener, was
convinced it was all a ploy on my part to escape
washing the dishes. Over the years, although I read
poetry I didn't produce much myself. I certainly got
hugely inhibited by the male English canon in my
years at UCD. Nevertheless I continued writing,
particularly after meeting Blanaid Salkeld, who was,
I think, the only woman poet writing in Ireland in
the 1950s. But, when I had a poem published in the
Student Magazine, like many a woman before me, I
chose a pen-name rather than my own.

It was only after I had raised 5 children that I felt
the strong urge to write poetry again. Now, I write
mainly from my own experience, and from a female
viewpoint. In Irish, I tend to write from a persona
also, but one to whom I feel so close it is almost
indistinguishable from me. I still feel something of
my 'Skylark' experience when the unborn poem
starts in me as a rhythm, an unheard music, with no
subject matter, and a chaos of words or images
somewhere just beyond my grip waiting to have
order put on them.

contents

EMIGRÉ

Sometimes I leave my natural body,
migrate to new spaces - virtual worlds
where meanings are not anchored,
the flesh loses its moorings,
and the cursor shapes the might-have-been me.

To-day, somewhat tired of exile, I have
a gut-need to return to my physical self,
hold on to something more tangible,
paddle sure conduits to bedrock,
search out where a thought might grow
as in the dark damp places where crystals are born.

THE BURNING

(Bridget Cleary was burned to death in her own cottage on 15 March 1895. She was murdered by her relatives in the belief that the 'real' Bridget had been abducted by the fairies).

Given half a chance, I could sleep off
the wretched cold I've caught
but I daren't close my eyes
for they mark me at all times
like carrion crows, beaks at the ready
waiting to skewer me.

I can see deep into their hunger,
the way they slaver for my blood,
crowd in and gawp around my bed,
bent on flushing out the changeling
they'd like to think bedevils me.

Not one iota have I changed
and well they know it.
It is they who have become strange
claiming, all of a sudden
to see this spiteful otherness
that inhabits my skin,
watches them from my eyes.

The fairies have white blood
in their pale-skinned bodies.
Monthly I can vouch that mine is red
though I've prayed God not to see it,
stormed heaven to fatten my belly with child.

My husband has persuaded
my own kith and kin to his side
swearing he has seen me
rub a shilling to my thigh,
that I sit on my secrets
with the smug look of a clocking hen,
don't open my prayer-book any more,
that I meet my egg-man-lover
in secret on the low road.

They put me to every test in the book,
hold me by the ears,
wave red-hot tongs in my face,
parade me back and forth to the hearth
dangling and smoking me
like a flitch of bacon over the fire.
They pour beestings warm from the cow
down my throat, prise open my teeth
to push in bitter herbs from a spoon
and the raging pain in my head
explodes like a star-burst.

Do they think to control me?
Judge me too big for my boots,
begrudge me my gold ear-rings,
the straw-hat made by my own hands,
my green stays, my striped petticoat?

The men circle me like marauding dogs
a sheep. No prayer of mine can shield me
from the lamp-oil pitched at me as surely
as they'd pitch slops into the yard,
no prayer can turn aside the tongs
and the flaming sod that sets me alight.

Will nobody help me?
Outside, I hear the clear bark
of the vixen from the rath.
She has fox-earth wherein to hide
and I have nowhere.

I see their frenzied faces,
smell my cooking flesh,
hear my own scorched screams
beseeching high Heaven for mercy.
Into thy hands, O Lord ...
From the maw of Hell deliver me ...

Their chanting roars like a gorse fire
tonguing the dark spaces
between my bones: *Away with you;*
come home, come home,
Bridget Cleary in the name of God.

Swifter than snipe-flight
over the Ballyvadlea fields
I am thrown headlong
onto a storm of tangled manes
and thundering hoofs;
my hair fuses with the night,
my eyes spark off every bog-hole.

IN THE NATIONAL ARCHIVES

Being dead before I was born
they became storied figures
elusive as veins of gold that sleep
in rocks, ancient flutes that after
centuries still hold a tune for me.

Turning reverently, one by one
each thick-leafed census table,
my eyes are torch-beams swaying
a zigzag path over the years
to where great-great-grandfather,
unable to read or write,
signs his witnessed X on the page.

I trace the light strokes up,
the heavy strokes down,
take some curious comfort
from the odd blob and erasure
that breaks the enumerator's
masterly penmanship.

Each name takes shape before me,
bodies not of flesh and bone
but formed by lamp-thrown shadows;
the great-great-grandmother, who could span
her waist with two hands when she came
a bride to this house with her dowry
from skivvying in New York,

her flamboyant husband, whose wit
drew the neighbours nightly to their hearth,

staggering home in the small hours
drunk from Keady fair;
their seven living children
and Henry, the dead baby, whose name
had got lost in the years, a small ghost
peeping through an erasure.

Another great grandfather, a cattle dealer,
summons his daughter home
from finishing school in Wigan Convent,
so he can afford to send his son
to the Holy Ghost's in Blackrock
and she married a man, handsome as Parnell,
bore him seven sons and two daughters
and dreamt of Wigan Convent.

I pick my way through their townland
hung about with damp cloud,
intrude on the earthen floors
of their friends and neighbours,
linger over scarcely remembered names -
McElvannas, Rafterys, Cassidys, McBeths,

but they give me no quarter,
steadfastly resist resurrection
and fade into their grudging fields
consigning me to a cold purgatory
where the eternity between me and them
becomes as empty as the space
between the stars.

ÉTÁIN

Distracted by a nide of pheasant
rising from the ice-bleached grass,
I never saw her land beside me,
crimson wings flaunting this January day
settling where the wind blew her
between clothes-line and laurel tree.
From what butterfly house had she
escaped? What bright Étáin
from the Underworld
had come that I might swallow her,
let her be born again in mortal form?

She belonged to no season of nature,
had no awareness of the comfort
of hyssop, conviviality of wings
on the buddleia, the flurry for position
in spring hedgerows and daisied meadows.
Distracted by a nide of pheasant
rising from the ice-bleached grass,
I never saw her go
leaving me with traces of crimson
around my mouth,
throat full of wing-rush.

ABOUT BEING HUMAN

It's knowing that we can match
bone for bone of ours with bone
of monkey, vole or seal.
It's opening our fin-like spread
of hands to the light; the need
to roost above stoat and fox,
walk among lions, close like oysters
around some pale seeds in us
that may take years to grow.

It's how we eat knowledge
in the way water swallows light;
look dreamily at acres of star-fields
where we've appliquéd whatever gods
we haven't abandoned to the murky fills
of ditch and bog. It's a hundred
tortoises in the Sultan's garden
candles strapped to their backs.
It's the death camps, the gulags, Hiroshima.

And to-day, as you drive away
to wherever it is you live, whatever
it is you do, it is your foetal cells
decades later still riding my blood.

WHITE FUCHSIA

We were walking in the De Vesci gardens
my mother-in-law and I
moving in brindled shadows
along ancestral avenues
of chestnut and oak and lime
to where lustrous magnolias floated
on a pale lake of sky.

We were walking in the De Vesci gardens
my mother-in-law and I,
like some curious caterpillar she
in furry coat and hat, grew palpably transfixed
by dangling leaves and spearing bulbs,
and all but swooned with the promise
of so many sprigs and shoots.

We lingered by the cooling pond,
my mother-in-law and I,
in front of the buttery
in the De Vesci gardens,
dipping our fingers in the pool,
watching its sunny waters splash
on the stone umbrella of a sculpted girl and boy.

I scarcely felt her leave me
in front of the buttery
in the De Vesci gardens,
not straying too far at first,
she ferreted for faded labels
like a short-sighted botanist,
then distancing herself imperceptibly
she seemed to fuse with the far-off trees.

I watched her come back along the path
clasping her stomach tightly
as if the gamekeeper had just shot her,
her handbag spilling over with greenery,
leaves sprouting from between coat reveres,
straggling from shallow pockets and bursting
from between bulging half-way buttons.

Fearing that we'd be turfed out
my mother-in-law and I,
arraigned in the De Vesci gardens
and shamed before the Sunday crowds,
I rammed her precious plunder down her bag
and caring not for node or bud
pushed back every telltale frond
from the margins of her coat.

That evening she laid them out one by one
wrapping each bruised specimen
in damp newspaper sheets
ready for the train journey back to Galway.
'And this is for you', she said
handing me a wilted cutting of white fuchsia.
'It'll be grand on the bank. Plant it
where you can see it from the window'.

These days when it is high summer
and she has long since gone her way,
the white fuchsia burgeons and tosses
an avalanche of commemorative bells
and we walk again in the De Vesci gardens
my mother-in-law and I
moving in brindled shadows
along ancestral avenues
of chestnut and oak and lime.

'THE BLUE DRESS'
(Henri Matisse)

He had to hate her to paint her
out of existence,
to cancel her out, imprison her
within great folds of cloth

voluminous sleeves
and rhapsody of frills
flouncing at the neck
elating the bodice
cascading in arabesques to hem.

Did he love her once
then froze her in this room
at some unclean time
lest at her touch
his world might fall to pieces?

And now he is master,
her nothingness complete.
The dress bubbles and flows
from compliant shoulders,
her hand a starfish in its depths.

'LADY VENETIA DIGBY ON HER DEATH-BED'
(Van Dyck)

Lustre and shimmer
of a grape-like bloom
on velvet drapery
that rumples and blends
into an opalescence
of delicate bed linen
where Venetia dies
supported on pillows
flounced with shadow

and posing for death
in her organdie night-cap
pearls at ear and neck
did the smell of paint rankle
as he worked to shape
cloth and bead and flesh
his palette grounding her
for the centuries
in this crepuscular room

did she sense clouds outside
push in from the west
the gauze of a windless day
shiver to evening
and the eavesdropping light
retreat farther and farther
letting her slip past herself
and his careful disorder
of rose-petals
on counterpane and sheet.

FALLEN WOMAN

He made visible the invisible,
coaxed her into being from molten glass,
raced against time to shape her space
until all the viscous honey of her
set rock-solid and translucent,
golden as amber drowned in Baltic seas.

If this be a fall, then she is all grace
her body propped on one radiant elbow;
head down, she might be studying red ants
or seedling heliotropes in the pink earth,
no Adam or God to witness that apple
clasped round and fat behind her back.

I shade my eyes before her incandescence,
try to interpret the scattered fronds
of an old language behind each refractive curve
and suddenly see, looped and coiled
in the belly of this unshamed Eve,
the serpent she has swallowed.

COLUMBINES

Inspired by a girl's frilly petticoat,
he put them in a bed, let them breed
where soil was so rank and full
the reticent double cream that started it all
ruched and flounced lime-green;
Ice-maiden, shimmying with Raspberry Ripple,
vied with the lush can-can of Strawberry Surprise.

He watched a myriad insects tunnel them,
heavy bees ransacking their sweetness
stagger out in the sun blinded with pollen,
observed how the flowers swapped colour
criss-crossing the bed to reinvent themselves,
their old artlessness consigned to some basal attic
they would be reluctant to unpack again.

Yellow was the black sheep, the dropout,
the flower-shape-flower-colour that eluded him;
abashed at having herself crimped like an apple pie
she turned the key on her frivolous wardrobe
gathered her plain skirts against the summer
and left in a tremor of legs barely covered
with a froufrou of dying leaves.

Memory of her grew more exquisite;
he sifted the seedbed in search or her
widened his net to take in grassy sheep walks,
damp places among bog orchids and shore dock,
even the dead nettles and charlock by the roadside;
he made a television appeal to gardeners:
Please if you get a yellow, I want her back.

Back at the bed with soil so rank and full,
he took to watching his blooms under the moon's
pestle
that compounded colour and shape to a buttery blur
gilding his own leathery hands to a sculpted beauty;
and he cursed the madness that fired his passion for
a flower
escaped from him way beyond the miles of cornfields,
where her luminous carpels swelled eternally yellow.

I SEE YOU IN AGE

Knowing too well that I've been here before
every impulse is to sidle
from a recognition of the way
the cover of familiar trees
truckling to a prying wind
blockades of sneaky briar-manes on the make
the glaucous light of summer.

Suddenly through a secrecy of foliage
I see you facing me again
not as in your hey-day but old
and wearing your desolation
like an abandoned house
barely breathing lest your final floor
crash from its joists.

WAITING TIME

Windows opened up for him
on some strange land
that the catheterised light
could not penetrate
and the white feet that padded
through his lengthening sleep
found no foothold
in the crevice of his days.

Only the waxen roses
chill under their glass of years
gleamed in the quiet country
round his heart
until his soul, a rock dove
found its ledge,
its shelter above my door,
for it rained
about the throne of God.

AFTER YOUR FUNERAL

Your apron - more of an overall really -
a splodge of blue and violet flowers on navy,
he washed, pulled into shape and carefully ironed
a matter of days after your funeral. I walked in
where it hung on a wire-hanger
smack in the middle of the kitchen wall.

I couldn't meet the eyes of a hundred flowers,
the six white buttons frosting the winter light,
the way the sleeves might be lifted to a cross-shape.
It was easier to think of you under a headstone
that the sea-winds and rain and ice
would shape, erasing to an unhurried blur
your little life-history written in stone.

Winter has come early to your room.
The last of your thoughts, indecisive stragglers,
collected themselves and took off weeks ago
with late migrating swallows
leaving you, once the tie-beam of this house,
agate-eyed, unknowing, staring at me
while I wait for you to smile, stand up,
say this is all a joke
and hurry towards me with outstretched arms.

The woman who cares for you
bustles in and out, saying *won't you sit down,*
but as you can see, she's not herself
at all to-day, not herself at all.
Earlier she has gentled you into this chair,
a rag-doll anchoring your restive hands
and wrapped you so warmly rug-tight up
not a draught from the yard can feel you.

You are lost to this room, to the photo-smiles
of your children and long-dead husband
beaming at you from mantel and wall.
In vain I search you out amongst them,
try to frame you in old summers
standing on tiptoe in the orchard
to fill your apron with apples
or walking the rough grass on the stanks
ankle deep in vetches and knapweed.

Sitting with you now a matter of minutes,
I grow uneasy under your gaze,
avert my eyes, not wanting to enter

that dark landscape where nightmare-like
you stray in the path of winds
I have no hope of following;
where you chase a myriad words
blown away from their moorings
and founder amongst well-loved faces
that shape and reshape themselves as strangers.

REPOSSESSION

In search of a place to rest your age,
(or should I say send you off to die?)
I start the engine, bear you down roads
alongside a watery sun low behind
winter shoots of willow and beech,
to corral your befuddlement
in a glumly-painted room
in an Old Folk's Home
in another town.

I desert you there in Indian territory,
Navajo to be precise, not that you'd know;
though your hands plane concentric patterns
of mudstone and shale, polish wings
of wheeling hawks and vultures on pages
of the National Geographic I've left you
while age, twisted, incontinent, miasmal,
watches you curiously from the door.

I find you seated alone to-day,
the dead-weight legs I couldn't budge
pyjama clad, your fingers tugging
at the catheter they have inserted
for the umpteenth time.
I read to you, show you family photos,
haul your spent brain after me.

It is useless. You've closed down. It is Sunday.
The matron just in from golf sits on your bed
teaspooning mush into your baffled mouth.
He was an educated man, she proclaims.
Who you are or were is lost to me these last months
but your eyes still turn in my direction.

The phone rings. Your face pale as a tussock moth
flies through the clearings and coppices
of my wakening. *If you hurry*, the voice says.
Ignoring your blue fingertips, pretending I don't hear
the scroop in your throat, your scantling breath,
I blow out the candle for the dying,
set out to repossess you, pleaching and bending
the years until I steal up on you
quite unprepared for you
to turn a formless face towards me,
bog-cotton hair a blur beneath your hat,
rag-doll legs flopping uncontrollably,
the sky primal and clouded with crows.

THE RIGHT TO DIE

Dying/Is an art, like everything else - Sylvia Plath

At first she clung to a sense of movement,
expanses of pavement rushing away from her,
her husband raking dead grass and moss
from the lawn she could no longer walk,
the waving repetition of reeds beside water,
rich raspberry monardias tumbling
before the early frosts of winter;
her young daughters dashing about the house
in clouds of conflicting perfume.

Her body paralysed from neck to toe,
she knew the currents, the dark side of rivers,
crocodiles brought down with the floods;
she knew the stars too, how some collapsed
like herself under their own gravity
their atoms imploding to neutrons and she begged
the courts to allow her husband help her die
before the final stages of the illness
that would surely choke and strangle her.

For a year and more, we edged closer
to a painscape so raw and intense
it made news headlines, filled our screens
as court after court rejected her claim
and we debated life, the meaning of being human
loss of dignity, self murder prepared within the silence
of the heart and a still capable brain,
knowing, that when death moved in for the kill,
there would be little art about her dying.

SHADOWS

This February day
a sapling-ash pans sunlight
through its branches,
riddling spangled shadow
on the rocky ground where I stand,
as though it would tease
that seeming dead stone
from its cold stare.
Two swans, their necks outstretched,
fly in rhythmic tandem upriver
where rudd and perch dart between weeds
and infant salmon wriggle to life
in their gravelly birth-streams.

Suddenly, I see my own form
cast amongst the shadows,
trace its broken outline
as I would a fossil in rock
knowing it is the stone
that finally holds the shape

and now like a magnet
draws the essence of me
into this landscape
where all my layers, flayed down
to something wordless
will not trouble a hedge-sparrow
nor cause a horse to bolt.

THE LAST OBSERVANCE

Here where the land ends
in a scattering of islands,
small stone-walled fields
cowering away from the sea,
light trembling behind rain,
we vigil by drenched rocks,
an eye on the turning tide,
waiting for you to decide
when it is time to move
in the last observance.

Gulls spill from the sky when
like a priestess, bare-footed,
in your black waxed jacket,
you step forward to prise open
what might be a lunch-box
except it holds the ashes
of your six-foot-tall father
borne by you to the Atlantic
all the way from a cattle farm
north of Brisbane.

I, who never saw the ashes
of the dead before, avert my eyes
not to intrude on your leave-taking,
study seaweed on the rock-line,
imagine to shape the man that was,
clavicle, femur, tibia and rib,
a tumult of bones I cannot name
and when I look again you are
already casting him on the tide

and it is whipping him to cream,
a galaxy of particles eddying,
whirling away from each other,
carried off before our eyes
beyond the shallows,
tugged by undercurrents
through channels between islands
to bed down with the bones of fish
and bird, niche between the eggs
of toadfish, lodge in a dog-whelk's shell.

This, his last wish fulfilled,
you say neither hymn nor
prayer for him but turn, face wet
with spray and tears, seeing
the long centuries of drowned stars
and moons like tabernacle lamps
hanging fathoms deep over him
and all of a sudden, you are longing
for home, the Pacific blue as a bird's egg,
the comfort of an opposite sun.

JUNE

Here toadflax sleeps in crannies of old walls
dandelions embed themselves in every cleft
hedge mustard roots at a lamp-post's base;
uncompromising weeds establish dynasties
as earth sprouts and spatters her ancient seeds.

You and I control well cultivated plots
where roses that for more than half the year
pruned back in beds to spiky skeletons
just now discharge great cabbages of bloom
that snag and bleed thoughts barely fingered.

Something from every luscious June we ever knew
absentmindedly nuzzles the senses
until each inch of us seeps cerulean
and we tie and stake forgotten flowers
to musk and damask memory

These, opiates that sustain our days
absorb us into vortices of such sweetness
that evenings find us like fossilised bees,
the last nectar of our summer honey-sacked,
grown quite solid in stony abdomens.

THE NEST

The wasp-man, garbed in space-man white,
face now unveiled, hands ungloved,
presents me with the nest, not whole
as when it hung last night
its blurred aura an unlit moon
silently stargazing from the garden hedge,
nor the time bomb it had become by day
the whirr and the throb of it threatening us.

For all I know, it may have been a bloodless
coup without as much as a corpse in sight,
the putty-coloured rind shattered
in a thousand feathery layers
white-edged like a cygnet's wing,
each larva cell hexagonal, perfect,
sculpted in spring, the wasp-man says
when crocus and daisy broke the grass.

I could bin my spoil; preserve it under glass
like a French bridal head-dress, but growing
uneasy with the sense of formless things,
with that something concealed in them and us,
those trapped echoes in endless birth tunnels,
the forever shifting pieces of our lives,
what fragile remnants we leave behind,
I consign it to an easement of leaf and earth.

DRAGONFLY GIRL

Summer evenings, voracious as any dragonfly,
she, with fine-meshed net,
hunts fields clammy after rain,
steals through grass and meadow-sweet,
purple loosestrife and marsh bedstraw,
bags cruising horseflies, mists of midges.
Startling small bats drinking from a pool
fringed with burr-reed and reedmace,
she strikes a bonanza of tadpoles, waterfleas
and the straggling larvae of gnats.

Hurrying back to the house with her spoils,
she thinks of fly-mouths poised to tear
limb from limb each pincered goody
squirming from her thin fingers
until glutted in their shallow glass lodgings,
their see-through wings spread wide,
their huge eyes waiting,
they dream, if dragonflies dream,
of ponds, canals and lily-pads,
lush river banks they've never flown.

At dusk, she removes their muslin sky,
releases a delirium of wings
to take a turn about the yard,
their blue-green iridescence flashing
round her like showers of shooting stars
while they, knowing their confines never mutiny,
come back to her as to a circus ring-master,
fasten in her hair like slides,
stream tamely to her hands
content to be cajoled back under glass

never observing how when dark falls
she steps from her skin as from silk
propels herself from her window-sill
on wings almost too sheer for flight,
the moon yellow as a marsh marigold
glinting on the metallic sheen of her body
and she all eyes and rhythmic flight
patrols fields and woodland rides
a thing outdistancing herself.

MIGRANTS

Women walking in the rain
past bricked-up arcades
disappear on terraces
that break the brink of streets,
lose themselves
down mines of night.
Their lives seem ordered,
each fragment louvered,
overlapping exactly
to ensure concealment.

Women walking in the rain
past island beds of flowers
on drenched avenues,
construct and reconstruct their lives.
A mist of dragonflies,
they drizzle their wings
on dark water,
fly close to the skin
of unlearned rivers.

Now there is no going back,
their summer country unfolds
along abundant banks
where reeds rise from shore-wash
and fishes leap
giddy to their glinting spin
until like Daedalus
in this final temple
they pass to progeny
a memory of wings.

THE ACCUSED

Women are always blaming themselves.
inexorable niggles of guilt
like pins and needles irritate our memories
feelings of daughter, mother, wife
move in at a moment's notice
intent on a free-for-all.

In search of forgiveness
we force ourselves to tiptoe back
to the beds of dying parents,
caress their frosty bones,
stare into the winter of their eyes,
asking ourselves for the millionth time
could we have done more.

We take shortcuts through the years
to relive old betrayals.
Groping along half forgotten paths
to trysts with lovers long abandoned
we strain to catch the whispers
of their sidetracked promises.

We wake up suddenly at night
with husbands who batter us
with stillborn babies
all curled up in the dark of us
and conspire with ourselves
to parcel up our secrets
so that the neighbours won't know.

Ghosts of lost days taunt our inertia
haunting us with what might have been
if we hadn't been too late with words.
Now nothing can be laid to rest
no comforting confessional-shutter
slides its absolution.

La Malcontenta

Provoked by the purr of rumour,
he observes how, like a golden moth
his wife flutters towards festive lights:
the coquetry of the dance,
theatres abuzz with friends,
notices how, when he unmasks her,
her eyes honeyed with excitement
rush for cover
scurry from his censure.
He will not be gainsaid
in his judgement of her guilt,
his sentence banishment
to a retreat in the swamps.

There fretful with sleeplessness,
restive in the marshy silence,
where stone-pines and junipers
frustrate the sun,
the slosh of oars and boats
on the Brenta unnerve her;
mornings, her eyes stare
down the immutable years
rummage in a glory-hole
of memories so thickly bundled
she can neither sift her indiscretion
nor find her sin.

Unable to go backwards or forwards
resentment galls her days,
only her anger goes free,
breaks the sullen curbs of her prison,
crêpes with darkness

the pallid garden statuary,
settles in resentful pools
around panicles of roses
or fuses with forlorn river mists
that lip the moorings.
And at nightfall her eyes
scan the landscape
search for even one will-o'-the-wisp
over the long marsh grass.

THE MERMAID

Water seeped through the ground,
took them by surprise,
rose on them inch by inch
until set adrift
they detached themselves from her
and drowned in its torrent.

Moonlight puddled the lake-floor
where she lay half dazed
in the sombre cavern that gave her sanctuary
from whiffling currents
and brimming flood.

Ghosts of sound haunted her
plummeting downwards
from the scuffled surface
in a distortion of bells,
in the unremitting yowl and call
of otter and bird.

Soon her body grew roseate,
took on a fish-like sheen,
sprouted scales of green
and violet and steely blue
until she was salmon from head to tail

And her mind roared with oceans,
overflowed with black estuaries
and the patterns of water she would follow
away from the headspring
out to the salt green sea.

THE POET IN SEARCH OF A DRAFT

The dog days have gone
dumbfounded by pigeon wing-beat,
bombardment from the garden hose,
slurp-sounds fish make
as they canoodle sleepy insects
on the underside of lily-pads;
yet day after day, the sun still sings
its heart out, sedating the brain
until I cannot tell word from word
and the pen melts into the page.

I should have planned escape
the way you do before commitment
to a person or a poem,
instead of sweating it out here
becalmed in day-dreamy doldrums
beneath castles of white sail,
with no option but to drop coins
one after silver one spinning
over the side of a ghost ship
in the vain hope I can buy the wind.

THROUGH THE MIST

The sun has no victory to-day,
cannot burn through the mist
that drapes itself between me and sky
so that I am enclosed membrane-like
in a frail womb-dream

where trees stand primeval
as in the brooding vapours of creation,
watchful crows sit vulture-still
and cattle loom gigantic
as mastodons in a museum.

This is where my past and present meet;
a dismal no-woman's land
where I must reshape my narrative,
pursue that alchemy of words which fly
like golden weaver birds to thread the page.

Meanwhile, I listen to the distant whistle
of thrush -call, guiding me for all the world
like those fishermen's wives on the shore
who whistled their menfolk safely home
over the misty sea.

CHIAROSCURO

These drab days after the solstice,
I chase the rationed light, search skies
for a stretch in the evenings,
strain for a tremor of spring in birdsong,
plan gardens of verbena, honeysuckle
and fragrant lavender to pillow
the returning sun.

Why then am I drawn towards shadows
the way hoarfrost clings to the unlit lee
of stone walls or ivy prostrates itself
in the shade under beech and oak?
Why do my eyes run with the vixen's
footprints black in the snow,
linger on the tracery of veins
that cloud your pale skin?

WINTERING

I follow the map of this winter
as I would the spirals on a nautilus shell;
the debris of hill and mountain
washed down by wind and rain,
leaf lanes on river and stream
drowned by uprooted trees in the flood spate,
seep of gap and ditch and field,
every drain filled with deadfall -
the black gunge of earth and leaf -
until this morning, opening my door
to a yardful of thrushes
cavorting in puddles on the tarmac
I felt words slowly awaken in me
like the cramped legs of bees
unfolding from winter sleep.

CHRISTMAS

We hang all our Christmases
one by one on this ritual tree
unchanging in the window-bay
shut out December
that bares itself again
like an ancient skull
a begging bowl for sorrow.

The kitchen mists with reminiscence
lost worlds of childhood
emerge and recede
wraiths in the steam of uncovered pans
old voices put to flight
in the scattered music of bells
that tune our skies.

Here with the sacrificial bird
iridescent on every plate,
amid chaplets of holly
we celebrate our liturgy
the nub of our love
oneness of our kin
lit by the candle's long flame.

The Saint

His eyes were the graves of stars,
black holes foxing time and space,
for he, bowled over by solitude,
had lived long in desert places,
fed on wild garlic and bitter herbs,
starving to a hermit gauntness
till he felt the power to work miracles
rise in him.

At Regensburg, he crossed the Danube
towards us on his threadbare cloak,
banished rats as big as hares,
lit fires with icicles, healed our sick,
baked us loaves of bread from ashes.
Sparkling drops from his fingers
became bees and the corn ripened again
under his blessed gaze.

Rumour has it he is a king's son
on the run from his own unworthiness,
who, seeing nothing in his body
but food for ravening worms,
untangled himself in the small hours
from the lavendered linen of marriage-bed,
the long hair of his princess bride
and fled the castle walls.

These nights bedded on nut-shells,
head pillowed on stone in his forest cell
under monstrous oaks where wild pigs
rootle for acorns and wolves lie
like lap-dogs at his door, we wonder

what maggot-host he must summon
to devour the memory of a girl's flesh
stubbornly leaching through that no-man's land
somewhere between awareness and sleep.

FORSYTHIA

Bright minarets of bloom
Yellower than summer pollen
Forsythia fills my room
Forsythia from a jug watching me

Yesterday it blew on a wet March tree
In a cold March sky
Now captive quiet forsythia

Shadows spattered by a wintry sun
On walls on floor on polished wood
The copper kettle spatters on the stove
Spattering all my sky
Forsythia makes wild whoopee
In bungee leaps groundwards,
And mounting the wind soars free.

Because Of This We Will Talk Of Trifles

Up there is a grove of talking trees
sun dappled pine, smell of their needles
crushed in the earth, threading memories
around me, through me, in me.
Pine. And another April laces
greening shadows along the ground,
moss-soft another Spring races
scudding past the trees, soundless
as clouds, quiet as an unvoiced dream.

We walk there through the pine plantation
you and I and talk of this and that
till dusk falls on our conversation
and time is something to wonder at.
What, seven o'clock already?
restless with the rhythm of unborn words
I look, and you are the Spring in me,
you are the pine and the words unheard.
Because of this we will talk of trifles.

THE FOX

Once, when I was twelve, she fed me red jam
on white bread in a basement kitchen
where light leaked through the grid,
probed her face, squeezing it
like the caterpillar cocoons I squashed
from the overhang of window sills.
It targeted her dead husband's portrait,
the wounded eyes that wouldn't leave her.
Tommy was a hero, she said,
had been on the run and died for Ireland
she said.

I thought of the fox I had got to know
slung around some woman's neck
at Benediction on Sundays in St. Mary's,
how I would stare into his sad eyes,
smell his soft , moth-balled fur,
imagine him red and running with life,
the hill-side bracken catching his coat,
making fox-earth ahead of the pursuing hounds
until the time he didn't
and became a trophy around her neck.

CAT MELODEON

Still following cat-paths
you trampled on the grass,
mapped out over twelve years
beating the bounds,
consolidating your kingdom,
I arrive at old haunts,
see you again in by-play,
all marmalade and foxy gold
stalking in the ravelled light
beneath the polished leaves of the Balloon tree.

From these prowling grounds
where once you guttled
on pigeon, magpie and thrush,
ravened after pigmy shrew and rat,
you used to vanish for days
on some hole and corner business,
coming back as befitted you,
aloof, enigmatic, tattered,
your slit-eyes shuttering
on demon ogres, rescued princesses
and palaces where you hobnobbed with queens.

O cat, Cat Melodeon, Melodeon Cat,
no more for you the *pas-de-deux*
at dawn with an Autumn field mouse,
brawls with the Abominable Snowcat,
the bravura of the kill.
Asleep in your last resting place,
with *langue du chat* leaves as canopy,
I sometimes swear I see your shadow
on the path, and branches of the dogwood
parting to draw you in.

HUNTING HAWKS

How often this languorous summer
we catnapped in shadows
cast by the house
half listening to the beaks of wrens
winkling insects from tree-bark
or a frolic of sparrows
fritter away energy
in a communal dust-bath.
Until yesterday when all alert
we watched a pair of hunting hawks
scribe circles on the sky
then beak-dive soar and disappear
behind the tallest oaks.
We never thought to warn
those nit-wit bathing birds
whose summer ended in a scream.

ADVENTURERS

Masters of our world
they dive through inky holes
of unknown seas,
measure, take photographs,
rummage the hideouts of gods.

Or livening up their Sundays
they squeeze themselves
through chinks in limestone,
drop into earth's secret basement,
swim her lost rivers.

Travelling north by shadows,
garbed in Arctic fox
and the skins of bears,
their faces stare us
from old autochromes.

Warriors of the maelstrom,
they pursue their Valhalla
through seas of grinding ice
across the final latitude
to plant heroic flags.

How they taunt the acquiescence
that snuggles us here,
our greatest finding
a long sought chanterelle
concealed in underwoods,
or gold dusted wrensong
from a summer hedge.

THE RECTOR'S DAUGHTERS

A grey nineteenth century day,
the sea-swell grey under sombre cliffs;
two sisters in a row-boat, small stick figures,
beneath a swooping , wreath of gulls
tow a trawl of seaweed, jelly fish, wafers of bone,
secrets of the empty carapace they will probe,
sit up late by lamplight, aching with the need
to name, label, paint in the most careful detail.

Sticking to the known to sift the unknown,
they never go missing like their brothers
in African jungles or Arctic ice; knowing
as they do by heart, the salt marshes of home,
drainage creeks where coastal and inland
vegetation merge, wildfowl and rabbits graze;
where keen as oyster-catchers, in the shore-wash
they gather here a fish-fin, there a fanned shell.

On the headland, the local women spread
seaweed and sand on a lime starved scatter
of potato fields, bleach their dull washing
on fuchsia hedges, sort slates in slate quarries,
suckle children, bury them, beget more,
watch the daft goings on of the Rector's daughters,
without as much as a husband or child between them,
breeding family after family of jellyfish in glass jars.

THE PLANT HUNTERS

Windchill plummeting like spoon-bait,
they press on with Sherpas and ponies,
pitch tent on some icy plateau,
hammer stakes into frosty ground,
hunch around camp fires drinking cocoa,
sharing bread and lumps of goat's cheese.
Nights, they dream cataracts of anxious dreams,
creep up on this genus or that
of rare magnolia and rhododendron
waiting to be bagged on the Milke Danda.

Snowsuits bright as fluorescent larvae,
they burrow out from their tents at dawn,
see clouds tined and separating
on a lactescent sky; go off stravaiging
about the site in seeming easy fashion,
eyes skinned for species of gentian
anemone, primula or Himalayan poppy,
then come to a sudden astounded halt
before *Paeonia sterniana* and all its pods
round and fat with the longed-for seeds.

From branches over raging torrents,
they dangle in nose-dive position to reach
into crannies for the last outlying plant,
and retreat with the sang-froid of circus acrobats
to list, label and pack their cache of seeds,
voices carrying like whooper swans
through the pincering air, impatient now
for glasshouses and the walled gardens of home,
for the drift and surge of blooms named after them
unfolding for them a fragile immortality.

THE COLLECTOR

Years later I can still recall
the sun-circle in the garden, the house,
how his old face beamed
when he pointed out his specimens
as though they were prize marrows
or a frippery of exhibition dahlias
acclaimed at the local show.

Not for him your neat rows of stamps,
pinioned butterflies or stuffed birds
frozen in flight under a glass sky
but the shrivelled body of a toad,
a dog's heart pierced with nine thorns,
a sparrow fastened in wax
wedged in the toe of a red high-heeled shoe.

I can still recoil from his real show stoppers,
tar covered foetuses romping from a wand,
the mummified corpse of Ursula Kemp
bumped off for witchcraft in 1582,
the skeleton of one Joan Wytte
the Fighting Fairy Woman of Bodmin.

All the long years of his delving,
knowledge scraped from the cauldrons of memory,
thumbnailed now on so many white cards
that conclude a world out of balance,
an ancient craft exorcised by new priests
muttering Latin and ringing bells.

Years later I can still remember
the half nude manikin splayed on an altar,
how she eyed me through a dark mist of hair,
how ribs of shadow danced on the sun-circle
shape changing to deviant shape
beckoning me. How I refused the dance.

THE WITCH

Here in this secret land
where moths pass
between me and the moon
and subterranean slugs
burrow in the white flesh
of late potatoes,
I tread luminous paths
drooled out by snails,
hoping to catch sight
of their sly coilings,
ferret out their mishmash of eggs
from cold wombs of soil.

Here I am all witch.
bats cruise in my shadow.
the stake where I burned
blends with my ashes
on an indifferent wind;
the waters that betrayed me
now float only leaves.
Here in this place
I no longer need to rub myself
with unguents of monk's hood
or anoint myself with belladonna
to fly through insipid skies.

CONCEALMENT

All is cloak and camouflage
in these sulky valleys
where the last bristle fern hides
and birds of prey hunt the land
where grass grows in a rank mat
layered on an eternity's compression
of wood and teeth and bone
and dendritic stones cheat the eye
masquerading now as moss
now as the most delicate trees.

Your skin too is creamy chalcedony
gleaming in the muslin light
of early morning
lining the crevices of wakening
coating over fissures of memory
so that I am afraid to touch you
half expecting that like petrified wood
in your search for concealment
you confused the disguise
and quite overreaching yourself
turned into pale rock while we slept.

THE PLACID SURFACE OF THINGS

Nature is such a sly colluder
spreading riots of weeds and wild flowers
over the rubble of old wars,
sending heather on the rampage
through spurs between valleys
where the bones of our forebears lie
jaws clamped on memories
of legendary paradisian apples
and all the while, we with our passion
for repossession, refusing to be hoodwinked
by the placid surface of things,
unpick bone and charcoal, fossil and shard,
hunt landrace oats on fallow headlands,
plunder the boscage of derelict churchyards
questing the crimson clusters
of a centuries-old rambler rose.
We construct photokit pictures of lost tribes
battered by Nature into changing course,
capture their primitive features in new faces,
pore over their shattered odds and ends
as if they were the holiest of relics
and wrench back the last scroop
of a dying language from an ancient throat.

To-day, keeping up the pretence
Autumn lays bare our dogwood
down to a brilliance of carmine bark,
never copping on how I hear its roots at play
with the glass marbles and jarrows
strayed from my children's fingers long ago,
never expecting the hard earth to yield
and toady before my retrieving spade.

Between St. Paul's And Smithfield

You watch them for years by the quayside,
their grace of frontage drawing the eye
to notice how their windows seem to wince
at the dereliction that degrades them.

Begrimed lace curtains press on glass
smudging out a gentility of rooms,
an intricate harmony of plaster
moulded for a gentler life and caste.

You watch them for years by the quayside
until one lunchtime, unannounced,
dangling from the necks of giraffe jibs
the demolishers swing their axes.

You try to dry-clean your conscience,
platitudes crowd your mind.
So the old gives way to the new!
They even knocked Van Gogh's Alcazar!

They are felling houses by the quayside,
jettisoning them from time.
What dripstone now will shelter us
from the rain of tomorrow's guilt?

THE RAIN-BARREL

I will raise the lid of the rain-barrel
and listen to the cobwebs strain apart
see the black spiders of the barrel dart
I will slam the lid and go.

Days long ago leaning over the edge
we laughed with the water children and stared
straight through their dark eyes and long droopy hair
their silently laughing mouths.

Rainy days and the water splashed cleanly
racing the narrow-mouthed iron chute
chased rain-drop-one-drop all in loud pursuit
till the barrel children hid.

They hid and died and if I raise the lid
I'll listen to the cobwebs strain apart
see the black spiders of the barrel dart
I will slam the lid and go.

CARNAC

Here light is low and even,
shadows, purple as meadow rue, lengthen
where breezes come a cropper
amongst a thousand standing stones,
runic patterns of lost enchantments
raised, for all one knows, to flatter and bribe
an exaltation of inconstant gods,
or aligned to track starsets,
watch crescent moons pull away from the sun,
ensnare the secrets of its vanishing tricks,
its corn-ripening, life-giving beams.

In the *Archéoscope*, we're like beachcombers
sifting light, riddling sound and special effects.
Fleshing out sheaves of long forgotten bones,
we breathe our Neolithic parents back to life,
lean with them against Atlantic gales,
fish their speckled salmon pools,
farm their clearings, herd their flocks
and tuning to old earth rhythms
trace the map of ley lines they sensed
beneath bleached grass where they hiked up stones
to soar above the restraining curbs of clay.

They are lying in wait when we go out.
Blurred syllables never set down
on wax or stone to tell their thoughts and feelings,
now settle on us like bloom on September damsons;
voids of old eyes spiral into us
until we cry out for all it's worth,
yes, we remember, you passed us a knowledge
of wheat and barley and podded things,

gave us sickle and plough, loom and wheel,
but why unload this restless dream of somewhere
where stone and tortured spirit meet?

[*Archéoscope*: Heritage centre at Carnac where the history of standing stones is traced]

DAMAZAN

This lucent evening, driving
between fields of blackened sunflowers,
we see the chimneys of that ancient house
outlined against an idle sky,
the courtyard watched by shuttered windows,
their tongues hanging out for a sup of paint
and Madame, a dishevelled wood nymph,
come laughing towards us from the trees.

Madame laughs a lot; leads us
over acres of faded carpets to our room.
Interlopers, we stare into old pantries,
shelves lined with quince and peach,
sneak looks at flagstoned kitchens,
derelict rooms, and feeding on her privacy,
abandon ourselves to the great mahogany bed
under the royal smirks of Louis Phillipe and queen.

Let the house children, who once day-dreamed
on nursery floors, plead with us wordlessly;
let Madame's ancestors stalk us for all they're worth,
they are displaced at this polished table
where she ladles out soup from a great tureen,
dishes up roast duck, pours wine from ruby glass,
her laugh, all the time echoing in the chandeliers,
an amulet against this nightly assault on her house.

ENLIGHTENMENT

It is *Maka Bucha,* full moon in February,
the day the Lord Buddha was born.
Every spirit house breathes in
some formless escape once trapped
in flesh under a beating heart;
cockerels crow from distant yards
and girls with flowers in their hair
make their way to the temple.

All is saffron-coloured cloth, garland
and incense where the Buddha image
glows serenely in his gilded skin,
rosebud mouth a tranquil curve
over long tongue and forty unseen teeth.
I try to grope the path to enlightenment,
lit darkly as in a dense forest,
feel every atom of me ball like quicksilver
and drop silently into a nothingness
way beyond pain and reincarnation.

I pull back from this void in the nick of time,
go outside to where evening draws in
around an old woman squatting
amid wicker cages of sparrows;
I want to release them all but buy two,
feel their small hearts flutter against my hands
then spread their wings, fly upwards
and look down at me from a *Bodhi* tree
free to roost in the sun's last rays.

I have made my kind of merit.

WAT CHANTARAM

Barefoot, I tread a path through his dream,
a forest of crystal pillars that reflect
themselves in an endlessly replicated world
where light shoots and ricochets
off a million mirrored tiles
until I am everywhere I look
the dreamer nowhere. And then I spot him
in his glass coffin on the high temple altar
lying among garlands of marigold buds
and sweet smelling jasmine,
a yellowed ivory shade trapped in lines
of light that bind him to his heaven.

I watch the day outside collapse
in rings around the temple dogs,
think about light, the seeming eternity of it,
how it too dies; about people I knew,
who took life in armfuls and burnt themselves out
like meteors leaving no dust
the cousin in New York who laughed so much
at his own joke on a summer's day
he fell backwards from a skyscraper window;
the aunt who rode horses for a Marquis,
rolled in the hay with stable boys and went
through the fortunes of two men, brothers.

Later, when galaxies of mirror- mosaic spin
around me, leaving all the debris of a glassy heaven
at my feet, I count bats in thousands stream out
from caves, slow moon-rats rummage insects
in the leaves and I face into that night beyond me
where darkness drowns the dreamer and the dream.

VENUS DE LAUSSAC

The museum light shows you
faceless. Head to one side,
a hint of hair, no nose,
curve of mouth, not as much
as a hollow to cradle an eye.
You are all tumescent belly,
energies of the womb
swell you endlessly.
for you belong to phallic shadows,
have given birth to bulls
in caves so secret
not a field-mouse strayed in.
At your will, their women
brimmed with child;
you made germinant the mulish fields
where they scattered doubtful seeds;
you sweetened their wells
and still the torches blazed,
the gourd-drums beat
beseeching you for more.

Something in your bearing, little goddess,
puts me in mind of a girl I knew once -
like you, a Venus. High heels,
pencil skirt, swagger coat.
I recall her faceless,
as week after week she swelled,
all belly at the end;
never thinking to take herself off
to a house of refuge in the country
run by the Sisters of Charity
for girls in her condition.

And we, embarrassed, avoided her
as though her fertility were catching
and when her son was born
she called him Merrion Baggot
Fitzwilliam Leeson - a litany
of the Dublin street names
where she was forced to move
from flat to basement flat
in the face of her shame.

AT HOME

It is Saint Patrick's Day at home,
the fractured light buckling down
to boost a landscape scumbled with rain,
reed grasses and seeplands spearing green,
holy wells uneasily brimming
with a shiver of ancient presences.
Now step-dancers release rag ringlets,
don costumes wanton with embroidery,
tip-toe reels and beat out hornpipes
on improvised stages on the backs of lorries.
Now lapels sprout acres of shamrock
and the politician's spiel tapers off
in a furious skirl of pipe bands.

It is Saint Patrick's Day at home
and far removed we are as pilgrims
in a land exuberant with gods.
Climbing this mountain path far above
silk cotton trees and orchards of apricots
that dissolve into the valley floor,
leaving behind terraced paddy-fields,
ditches shimmering with mica,
and the pendulous nests of honey-bees
we quieten like a swarm tanged,
settling on this nectared summit
before the sacred shrine of Shiva,
his tika a scarlet blessing on our skin.

It is the festival of Holi here
under a cobalt blue Himalayan sky
itchy with the chafing of multitudinous prayers,
our guide chanting mantras of mountain peaks,

Ganesh, Shisha Pangma, Gangchenpo, Dome Blanc,
me standing catatonic in the sun,
mutating to a disembodied substance,
clinging to the thin lifebelt of human song
floating up from some distant farm,
until in cahoots with my flesh again,
saved from the lust of Heaven knows what gods,
I fight for breath mouthing my own litany,
Slieve Mish, Croagh Patrick, Lugnaquilla,
Slieve Snaght.

SPLIT

MÁIGHRÉAD MEDBH

I wasn't always Máighréad Medbh. I took that name when I was 30, because in this country women inherit their surnames in the male line. I wanted to make a point. That motivation lessened in importance. After 2 years of self-consciousness, I couldn't imagine being called anything else. I had left behind the previous life. I was closer to what I wanted to be.

What do I want to be? Someone who lives creatively. I want to use my inspirations as well as I can. I don't say 'writer' although I plan to write always and to write better, because my experience with words is not just about writing. I associate poetry with dance. I try to write poems according to the music I'm hearing. I don't want to get boggy with syntax or soggy with illusions, although I'm very conscious of both. I want the subject matter to swell the sparse construction, as a body does a dress. I want to let the experience speak for itself.

I was born in Newcastle West, the homeplace of the great Michael Hartnett, and the heart of Norman Fitzgerald territory. Poetry was all around and although I wasn't conscious of its influence in the early days, I always had words in rhythm in my head. In common with most houses in Ireland, there were frequent recitations and songs. The accordion was taken down now and again, and my mother would force a tune out of it, although she asserted that she couldn't play. I don't know if it was the musicality of Irish poetry that did it, but I have never quite known where the poem ended and the song began. The vocal delivery was always important to me. Formally, then, most of my poems are conscious that they may have to be said or sung sometime, so they're prepared. 'Abair amhrán' becomes 'can dán'. Significant form is of the essence, and mostly I write in sequence. After all, it takes a long time to understand things properly. You may say it with the collaboration of your rationality, but it may not reach your body for a long time. What I want my poetry to do is to draw meaning from and to the body. When the hairs rise, I've succeeded.

contents

note

Some of these poems were previously published in *Poetry Ireland Review*, *Out to Lunch* (Bank of Ireland Arts Centre 2002) and *Riposte*.

I ...

is always in danger of toppling.
We bolster it upholster it
strap it around with a gun belt
and pin it with ropes.
This babel tower leans according to the wind
tries to imagine itself in another place
with a different style of window
but it can't leave.
Its one leg can only stand or fall.

.

INIS

The first time I felt home
was when the plane veered down on Inis Mór,
riding the airtufts
butta butta bounce
stomach over the mattress tucks
out feet and hip happy landing
on what is almost an airfield
low grey and wrapped in meditation.

First time I felt the memory of ground and let it be.
Didn't want to stamp all over it
and guillotine its daisies,
pluck the seeking parts from primroses,
or tear strips off struggling green swords.

I wasn't dressed for the occasion.
Jeans and a sweat-shirt -
not on in an air-heat of 22C.
My human friend remarked it,
she in her neat pink shorts
and barely strapped tight top.
Must have been an honest streak
struggling to marble my skin
and let her know, let them all know
I wasn't one of them.

Small way to rebel.
Another I thought was to squeeze possibility
from bone-dry situations.
Two fishermen and a philistine like me,
an insect hugging itself.

All things return to some centre in the end,
but not now.

Must be said I neared the circle there,
seated on the fishermen's sea-shafted benches,
eee of treaded boards and aaak
and fish whiff in the shifted boxed air.
Sing us one of your shanties.
The song a check of space and fill space and fill.
Your language is your viewpoint,
your own defining spot.
They see me *as Gaeilge*
I see them in English or Hiberno-English.
Makes your face a different shape, does it,
the language it's seen in?
If the fills are language,
what I want to learn is what the spaces mean
and if I could ever fall through them
to the oblivious, omniscient sea.

oh bear me home
oh bear me
where I am cloned at every pier
and mirrors of myself stare out
the sensitives of shale and stream

The next time I felt home
was when my chin on Charlie's shoulder
said, 'Don't move me. Let me snuggle, eyes closed'.
And bored though I should have been
with a hug so long and unchanging,
I took my time of his Atlas side,
his far-flung buoy,
felt the memory of flesh and let it stand.
Didn't try to bottle it in formaldehyde,

take it to a lab,
to a scalpel and a tweezers
and a place in a book of syndromes.
No.
I let him sail for a while
a cup called love,
a vessel named victory.
She might have made it.

oh bear me home
oh bear me
where I am cloned at every pier
and mirrors of myself stare out
the sensitives of shale and stream

BLOBS

because if you wake up and the room is a mixed-
media abstract with no centre and no-body's there
so you can only talk to yourself but you haven't any
subject so how

there's so much silence in the world feel it in the
mornings in ireland even on o'connell street dublin
where they all seem to know where they're going

can picture very little lying here despite birdsong i
suppose my imagination is small can only see a
desert and me in the middle spinning like an lp
with the speaker switch on tape

then there's so much chatter and that's silent too
the radio tells me a million things it thinks i should
be interested in and i don't know if i am or not
eventually everything ends up in an i don't know
because what do we know of anything

that's the reason we need sentences and
punctuation the reason for clocks suits stylish shoes
and ceremonies the why of hobbies and a working
day so we can forget that we haven't a clue what the
meaning of it all is

if we didn't have that order we'd end up lying in the
morning no beds or anything and we would be
blobs wouldn't we

CHILD

I could blame an army for torturing my child
and, true, they did pulverise her.
They came with lances and stuck each other
as she lay weakened on her back,
letting their blood drip into her open eyes
and their horses' hooves
stamp a demon mask about her nose.
They played out their lives on her,
using her as a stand for their games -
chess, poker, pontoon, roulette.
They split her like the atom.
She became a flash of beauty,
a joy for fifteen minutes,
a cherry blossom whose flowers bloom once.

I could blame them
but it's I who left her hungry on the open ground,
although she called to me
with a steelblade baby's cry,
although her face was in my image
and our history bulging her bones.
Well, it was a large plain and
without a map
friendless
I had no grid to guide my moves.
No-one answered you know
no-one when I called
as if nothing in that dimension knew my language.
I left her there,
pretending hyenas were friendly wolves,
fancying the sunburn on my arms was a kind of
pigment.

I drank with flowers of great sucking insides,
danced with satyrs who couldn't say foreplay
and young bears who tinkered with my nose
until it turned up blood.

I had forgotten the time.
Late again, never in synch with this place.
I saw them riding but hoped they would stop at the
farms.
Then they were at the child
and I had to learn by looking back
that all things need to be held
and fed their special food.
A child such as that
should have been suckling on my breasts to middle
age.

I recall her brief apotheosis,
when she was all spirit
and raced among the growing things,
naming them with sounds that crowned them.
She was perfect, but I was jangling chains.
I grabbed her one day in the middle of her dance,
for fear she would topple over the cliff she toed
and hauled her, shocked, back to shelter.
If she had cried more then, I might have given her
her head,
but she whimpered and settled for a twirl in a
corner of the hut.

I'm holding you now, Child,
who are blinded, armless, knees turned backwards,
your face a hoof-stamp and your memory wiped.
I'll display you on my lap,
where velvet will cushion you, and I'll sing you

something silly, something weighty, something sad,
some liberation song.
I'll dress you in royal colours and shapes of the
transcendent age,
knowing, Child, I have no other.

BINA

Bina still looks with a child's eye,
as she did on the day her uncle came.
It's all she can think of,
how the car whoa-ed up at the gate,
its redberry gleam, its sunroof.

She had to squint to see his face,
and then she stared at his white felt hat,
his windolene eyes,
salt and pepper suit,
yellow shirt and handkerchief.

He brought her a rose with a wandering heart,
silvikrin soft, seeding split ends
at the limits of pink.
He placed it in her palm,
called her darling, deemed her pretty.

That day the sun was her transporter.
Re-aligned, she spotted rabbits
and new flower-clusters.
Adults strolled by
with all the pomp of gods.

'Colour', she decided, 'is what I live for'.
She fixed at her waist her mother's scarf,
cardinal red,
a neat and decorous flag,
flaring triangle of desire.

He loved it. He drove her into town,
sat her in a bar and returned with a doll,
honey-haired,
velvet blue dress,
ribbon at the waist, white shoes.

She called it Celine and every week
brushed its hair to silk, washed the dress,
ran the ribbon
like a balmy breeze
across her pinking cheek.

Celine's eyes are postcard blue,
her eyelashes lush. Bina and she
sleep naked in the heat
of the same single bed,
flat chest to nipple.

The bedsit is full of summer flowers,
drawn in crayon or pasted on the walls.
When Bina goes out,
she shouts to the birds on the wire,
'This year, yee won't have to leave'.

She keeps close to the breathing hedgerow,
where she stands and remembers his suit and car,
his hand on her head
and the approving smile, never
repeated since she grew.

THE UNBECOME

Bridgie doesn't know that she's alive.
She carries her flesh like the dark load
heaped in baskets on a donkey's back.

She sees her likeness nowhere, nor her opposite.
When at times a mirror begins, she buckles with
fear
and smashes it before it becomes form.

Goes back then to where she has no name,
a place that when oblivious was bed,
but self-conscious is a spiked and contracting cell.

Evicted, she walks a narrow corridor
between name and its absence, not seeing the
others,
believing herself the only one without grasp

of this inaccurate map that is the body,
hiding from eyes that think they can define
her source, her measure and her meaning.

THE BEATING

It was a dense and vacant day, boiled as a bullseye.
Under the sky's big top all that was missing were
clowns,
a high trapeze, two elephants, three Pomeranian
dogs,
a lion, two tigers, a family of gymnasts from
Czechoslovokia
who also did the Tonto act, a ringmaster's whip.

Mistress of the centre-ring, I queened it over
buttercups and bluebells.
I turned conductor to the grape-green grass and
made it play
a fanfare as I skirted the scorching tar, directed
footsteps, knees high, back straight, toes rocketing
down.
Small birds dusted the trees and gave their eyes

to my little struts, my fine preening, my tail-coat
swagger.
Once in an hour a car would pass and I would
suddenly
sit, take a blade of grass and shred it, pensive as a
cat
with a dead catch. One time I forgot my public and
parade
and found myself by a neighbouring gate staring at
their curtains.

Missus wore her hair streaming, like a princess
turned from the castle, left wandering forever
without comb or

pillow to lay it under. She told us she had been beautiful,
had kept her trousseau in a lined drawer in her father's careful
house, but had married a serpent in disguise, her sister too.

Earlier on she had sat in our house and darned my brother's
sock, my mother's ruse to make her worried woman's
hands feel useful. 'He said he'll finish me off when he comes home'.
Beating the badness out of her, that's what she said he was.
An amateur exorcist circumventing men in black.

How do they train the circus animals? Pretty pomme dog
becomes puppet, elephant plastic, tiger in striped pyjamas.
A whack. I'm a reliable witness. An implement was used.
The leg of a chair I believe she said. And a scream and a whack.
The curtains swayed as if they wanted to start a show.

The circus ended. Still amazed, a sullen girl with tangled hair,
walking the ground where the caravans stood, looked for a trace
of the boy with the black eyes and gravelled skin. A crumpled

and discarded ticket became the souvenir she stuffed
like an insole in her ring-master's boots before she
turned away.

PURBLIND

They created the other in large fields,
where they paraded their majesty
before clapping crickets
and swaying bodies of grass,
butterflies rising like balloons
to celebrate their advance.

He knew that every night,
with whomever he married,
he would hardly sleep for love-making.
He would bring her gifts
and complement her hair.
She would be natural, no make-up or airs,
a motherly girl with such a mind.

She allowed the hands of a faceless college boy
to reach her in etheric regions of summer meadows.
They would lay for hours in spirit beds.
But the man she would marry
would be a tall provider,
who would lush her with clothes,
enrol her in tennis clubs,
feel her secretly on aeroplane seats.

Stepping like that, both purblind,
was it any wonder they met?
What groping hands tell is not a lie,
but the picture they draw
lacks the dialect of sight,
is a religion rather than a science.

Running from the fields
to neon with hearthflame in its nose,
they became what they thought they should -
coupled, manacled,
the planned freedom of fields
emerging to its image,
a prison farm,
which they will wander some time more,
burdened by the unappraising sky.

marriage An uneasy living arrangement between two adults and any number of children, wherein you may criticise the other partner endlessly, study their every move and constantly dissect their motivations. Sex may be had occasionally and you may feel their legs or private parts without asking. Advantages are a sharing of income, the fact that you are never completely alone and sex, as I've said, on occasion. Disadvantages are the same.

birth 1 An introduction to the physical world of sensation and socialisation. A kick in the arse that dislodges you from a dark warm place and cannons you into brighter lights than you will ever see again; strain on the eyes; a headache if you have been sucked; hunger and a scramble for someone to call your own. 2 A white blanket, lots of white and blue beings and every sound too sharp for your ears.

sex 1 Compulsive behaviour pattern common to 99% of humans and animals. An ache in the lower regions of the body confuses you as to whether it is pain or pleasure, but causes you to behave irrationally, engaging in frenetic activity with somebody you afterwards realise you must speak with. 2 A desperate and rather graceless act of near-assault on the body of another, spurred by a desire for release, which, if not achieved, ruins your day, and successfully reached may ruin your life.

eating 1 The act of cramming the oral orifice to a greater or lesser degree with masticable substances

for the purpose of sustaining the functioning of the body. 2 A balancing act wherein food must be spiked with a fork, manoeuvred with chopsticks or other illogical instruments, and placed in the mouth without mishap. 3 A type of social intercourse in which one must keep one's eyes away from the other's mouth and chew silently while keeping one's own mouth closed. Bad eating manners mean you will never marry or you will get the downmarket man.

studying 1 The act of staring for a long time at a book about a subject which does not interest you and has no bearing on your everyday life. 2 The pretence of reading such a book so that your parents leave you alone, and then replacing it with a copy of the latest teen mag. 3 Preparing the answers to a list of possible questions which you must answer in handwriting so that you will earn enough to support yourself for the rest of your life.

burning your boats Telling people what you think and, in so doing, losing friends and never obtaining a well-paying job.

dossing 1 A productive activity in which you relax all your muscles and drink yourself into a coma. 2 The act of staring soberly into space, speaking slowly and mentioning the word 'ideally' over and over again. May involve making molehills out of mountains, a dangerous task if undertaken without the correct equipment.

playing 1 Anything that involves shouting, jumping, bouncing, pretending and laughing.

Almost always ends in tears, injuries and stone throwing. 2 Also applies to games of rivalry, where two groups of adults are pitted against each other in the performance of meaningless but difficult tasks, such as the placing of a ball in the back of an upright net.

death The end of all the above.

FEED

Since the night you fed me oysters,
offered the smooth grey flesh on a casual fork,
and I wrapped my mouth around it,
sucked on the cool prongs,
took ice-cream too from your spoon
as though you had always been my feeder -
since then my mouth has moistened
at the thought of you,
and the thought has popped up,
jack-in-the-box, in the least convenient places.

I have pointed my nipples in your memory,
like church spires skewering the air,
and I intend, if you will allow,
to take you chasing the sky,
scraping it with your fingers
until you shower in your own cream,
your head invaded by tropical reds
and a thousand hummingbirds.

I always give gratitude, and to you for this -
that, snug in lycra-treated jeans,
I could swagger and flirt through the restaurant,
that your eyes gleam when they smile,
like chestnuts caught in a freak shaft of October
sun,
that you put your hand into a hole in the tree bark,
not knowing where the bees nested,
and when I grasped it, pulled me out
to where I could hear the possibilities of song
and not a wooded echo.

You're a straight speaker, gauche as a new-born,
a bit of a mouth in fact, but your observations are
astute.
Come back to me sometime with a hot worm
and drop it earth-red and stiffening into my beak,
while it's still wide and its stalactite dances
in imitation of that first movement with you.

BUBBLE

The moment you seized your tears is not past.
It has bubbled and flies over the houses in secret,
high enough to be mistaken for a tiny refraction of
light.

It was Sunday
and an empty space blooding in my head
caused me as usual to bang saucepans on the
cooker,
slam press doors after cups had been removed,
sit staring at the wall as though I were a locked chest
wedged at the bottom of the sea.

It was him I yelled at, if the direction was astray,
the tornado heading for you
and not towards the closed door where the body in
foetal pose
made a womb of the blankets.
Him I hated for his stubborn pitted silence
and the hard glass ball he spun around himself,
like a dried flower flattened into a paperweight.

So I shouted, may have brought my hand
screaming to the table where you inevitably sat,
having no other mother to go to.
You had cried before.
This time you began and then,
seeming to think of a new strategy,
contracted your throat and beavered the stream
at the edge of your lower lid.

The bubble hovers still,
waiting, I know, for some careless spire
or the beak of a long-flying bird
to splatter its innards in sprawling spiders
upon our heads.

ZOWIE

i can't leave him mammy
can't let him lie by daddy
zowie hugged me when i wanted
he's the only

i can see him when i close my eyes
he's legs up on the bed
always where i left him
staring at the ceiling

when you came to the door
your eyes were waterfalls
your voice was fast and scary
hurry hurry
you'd buy me all the clothes i needed
all my toys were scutty
you had money and a job
and a new boyfriend
car purring at the bottom of the street
your hand on my shoulder
like caster sugar on apple tart

it's been two years mammy
zowie in my bed
zowie in the dark after daddy
after he'd get me to pee for him
i told zowie everything

i'm running back
zowie's supergirl
my heart is like the world's biggest drum

i should be on parade
except i'm shy
and zowie's waiting
when i grab him i can hear his heart too
we're a band

hugging zowie
watching mammy
now we've got away
she fixes her make-up
seems just as afraid
zowie and me the brave

THE TUNNEL

We have no right to be sad
who have reached down throats
and squeezed hearts,
then left them to repair themselves
as naturally as they might.

Our tears are water but seep
through rifted landscape,
where everything that flows
disappears like ghost-sound,
unheard by most.

We cannot trust our grief
who have slapped our children
and seen their cheeks brighten
like bruised oranges,
seen their cheeks sogged as winter leaves.

We have no welcoming breast
because we have not shared our reason.
We take lone walks in deserted, buzzing kitchens,
go skinny-dipping in dead seas of beer,
where everything, scum or not, floats.

We have no real friends
because endings are what we understand,
and there are too few
who can do the tunnel
and survive.

TABERNACLE
(To the air of 'Venite Adoremus')

The altar of your temple
displays my tabernacle.
In velvet I inhabit the golden box.
Gilded and girded,
one-winged aviator,
bound to your slave-service,
waddling in a square space,
your peacock, your hunting hawk,
your whited host.

I'm weighted with your presence,
with diamond rings and pendants.
No bird could take to flight,
these stones on her feet.
Lay off the diamonds,
I can't help but reach for them.
I clatter to the glitter,
was born a breed of magpie,
I claw at you, draw some blood
but you will not leave.

If lonesome you would open
the arching wooden double doors,
I'd wing it through the slightest chink,
I'd make for the blue.
Springboard for space flight
to valley of the breached egg,
o-zone coruscating,
wires popped and functioning,
come welcome to nirvana,
Bird the Queen.

LION'S PLAY

What would I do rising from a sun-dream but make love to you as a lion? You bite into my hair not knowing where it orangeful came from when it had been clipped. It's all over the place now and you can't get away from it. You're getting electric shocks from it. You keep twitching and throwing small convulsions like you can't stay and you can't not.

I like my lion face. It's wide and still pointed. The nose is the best part. It sniffs, not ordinary sniffs like a human nose, but sniffs that smell long distance. I whiff the sprung spring of a man two miles away. Come back to you and your round bouncy water bags full of juice loosey feeling ready to spill yeah yawn. Lions always yawn I always yawn when I want you. Under the awyawning my legs are in a Y and all my lips are opening wide. Come into my maw my jaws. There's a nice prey. I'll throw myself over you coatlike and with great furry hands on your shoulders hold you down. You're mine I have you now you're not going anywhere. I'm coming onto you snaking you in perhaps bleeding you but you like it don't you. Plaything happy balls bounce bump reach for the main thing the upper echelons the top of the food chain nothing eating me now.

HUSBAND

You have put so much fluid in me now
I'm your jug.
You can lift me onto your head,
straighten your neck
and walk pole-backed from the village
to your home among the parched grasses.
Pour me out
and this silver stream will turn to mercury,
stretch itself, then mushroom up
and make a lion's shape
to frighten those bandit nomads
of desert, ache, distance, namelessness.

he's the one

... who stroked your back when the contractions hit
... who washed your blood-stained nightgown
... who worked for a ticket when you longed for the sun
... who takes you to meetings and waits outside
... who listens to astrology but knows his fate
... who says you're great when you're only good
... who buries hatchets while they're still sharp
... who stays in your bed although you have no desire

THE LITTLE THINGS

These are big things,
as big as mortgages
and our son's need for a winter coat,
as big as the job you must maintain,
must suffer morning traffic for -
you snapping at me in the morning,
I snapping at the boys in the afternoon,
you making me cry, I passing it on.
No wonder they goad each other.

The way I'm often tearful -
that's a big thing,
a thing to be understood,
to be prised for pearls
and not to be ignored
for fear of contagion.

These are big things -
your aching throat, your ocean of non-recall,
the stiffness of my arms when you arrive,
our armed dialogue and anxious-eyed skirting,
I lost and unbelonging on the windward side of the
bed.

It's a big thing
to struggle from bed with muscles in a bind,
hardly able to persuade the legs
that there's ground worth exploring.
Exploring is the biggest thing of all,
which your ticket to tradition will preclude,
and my childish need for a hand hold back.

RENEGERS

The faithful have sanctuary in this church.
The serrated altar has spread its wings
and nestles them in its heritage of stone and bone.
They have their place at the heart of the cross,
where suffering is always repaid with a golden key.
Gathered to commemorate a death,
they can claim their right to ceremony
and the unintercepted touch of the priest.

But we who have reneged,
who are wandering in the desert, heads high,
always the last to trust the mirage, though dry,
stand at the circle's edge, accepting
that familiar spatter of water from yesterday's land.
Our child stands to be part,
to follow his cousins to communion
and I whisper the message that he can't receive.

This week we liked a school
which Edmund Rice founded and O'Connell launched
because it smelled of rural teaching, a slow
walk, antiphonal certainty, pillars
and careful talk in hallowed book-lined rooms.
All prayer spreads old colours,
changing the air to plumb sounds and strata,
talks to the skin.

We have tried to transcend names,
some given, some flung, which render us small aspirations
in a collective noun. We are proud of our courage.
I take shamans for my friends,
spirit animals and Odin who becomes all things.
And walking into that room
where Edmund Rice prayed,
I sense all ashrams in the fire of my head.

No Day of Rest

The first was her face, that scattered a mouthful of
runes,
melon of moon relaxing, fetish on the carved back
of the sky.
Who could pass her on a cow-eyed small town
evening
whose skin said berries, milk chocolate
and wax polish long before Johnson's?
She could have been born by the Ganges,
would have complimented a stream of silk -
zardosi rippling over saffron, emerald, vermilion.
'The floor is good tonight', said Willie Burke,
his saddle shoes on her pointed toes.
'Yes', she laughed, 'You should try it for a while'.

The second was his resolve. Tightened to find a
wife,
take his bare feet out of the rusted can of the slums
and dip himself in sweet green swabs.
His heart did physical jerks and his stomach quick
twists,
corkscrewing itself like molecules of DNA.
At her brother's wedding he was military man,
latter day Oisín, Michael Collins and Tyrone Power
curried together in a mythical mutation.
She was his vision from the true side, his shining
door.
She would see herself yet in his glassed black boots.
He marched everywhere.

Two stories that brought them to church.
One that he pulled her down for a kiss under a
chestnut tree;
she later returned to break a branch off and parade
home
under its mistletoe palm, her dress capering around
her strong-boned legs.
The other, that a practical and aged aunt made their
match.
The first four born were large and consecutive.
He still in the army, they had their fill of Grandad's
generous hands
whose large sweeps could paint a child's tearful face
clownish again.
His visits were poisoned spears, suffering things at
the end of hard cycles,
twenty-six miles each way and a week of desperate
denial between.
He would issue instructions, master of his house,
absentee lord.

His temper tore slates off roofs, blasted chunks out
of walls,
gushed itself, insidious too, into the middle
chambers
of the ears of children who learn by hearing,
whose tears are always visitor to the swinging door
behind the eye.
I heard a child psychologist say such children could
be destroyed.
Three more birthed to the other side of army were
his,
less assured of their mother, who no longer bought
crayons
or taught them to pole-vault over the high gate
beyond the bridge.

Between rantings and upturned tables, he showed these children the galaxy,
one learning stars and planets, one a type of fatherhood, the last a paradox.
The sky seemed better blanketed than their shallow-mattressed beds.

He spoke of love as a manoeuvre and marriage a battlefield.
She named hers destiny, a fortune-teller's understanding,
and prayed it like a ceremony: 'If we don't love him, who will?'
The odd birthday he would fling a box of chocolates on the windowsill
and rush out. One wonders where the family learned romance.
They thought they had, and careered like rising streams
from the house at eighteen to plough the nightclubs and bars,
dominoes, one on the other, conservatives dreaming of drugs.
They were a psychic mafia, a fort no comer could disturb,
with their in-jokes, their mother's gutsy wit and their father's cold cut.
Everything, they assured the cynical, could be worked out.

The rosary strained, wouldn't keep them
honeymooned.
They found in themselves their father's tendency to
suspect, each other too,
their survival lessons learned so well they were
always old dogs.
Still, in a Clondalkin graveyard in October, the
furthest he got from home,
the loudest brother lay down in a hundred wreaths,
children and adults dissolved
in a mirroring pool. He had rainbowed the lives of
the wounded, donned the duty cap and kept the
home fires ablaze as if that were the greatest good.
They had buried their parents. They came again,
shocked, to bury and praise,
to stand, six siblings, at the unstopped gap of the
torque.
I, his most distant, could hardly leave, his body his
greatest part.
I was forgetting I believed in souls and not in
jawbones.

With family, love lodges in the organs. Watch for
where it hurts
and consider it made strong. My heart catches. His,
he overstrained.
Come to this point, where the paragraphs of
generation are compressed,
I can see you were right, brother, to declare no day
of rest.

Brown Terrier

There's a night to die to, brown terrier,
with Orion over the airport like the boss,
a foot on the runway,
a foot on the highest tree of the hedgerow,
nosegay of stars for his codpiece.

This is the clearest night yet of winter,
galley of spring in the appled sunset,
opening to a scrubbed night sky.

I drove through two red lights tonight
and careered up a one-way street.
It could have been me to knock you
and leave you huddled into your squashed body,
astride the broken line between what we know
and what we fear.

CLOCKMAN

This man
the clock has him beat
has him small and effete in the map of its hand
of its click and its twitch like a branch
like a cliff where he fell when he slept.
When he walks he is tripped by the black of the tick
of the cliff and the drop and the drip that he is
that he sees on the tap that he never got fixed
never got down to it picked up the phone
up the courage to say 'well hello, there's a clock
there's a tap doing claps in my head
in my house where I spend half the day
half the night maybe more wide awake
wide apart from my wife with the nails
with the fists of the clock on my chest'.
On his forehead halfway from the right to the left
to the north of his nose there's a line on the skin.
On the stroke of the hour comes a stab and it cuts
and it delves on its way to the front of his brain
of his will which is cleft between fighting and flight
and he knows when his mouth moves around to his eye
to his twelve to his top of the clock
it will bite.

THESE ARE THE FEELS OF SILENCE

1. Reach

The thumb raises itself
for no particular reason.
The air looks at it, rearranges,
then settles back into apparent sleep.

The air may be reaching in its way,
but the thumb is just a thumb,
represents nothing.
Another time it might have been a standing stone,

a king's stamp, the far half of its own ripple,
the teat of poetic mead.
Now it has no geography, no co-ordinates,
and because it cannot place itself,

it wouldn't matter if particles around it
fried with heat,
it would still shiver, abandoned
as the tower when Rapunzel had found her prince.

2. Look

There is some conclusion to be drawn from the sky,
but looking catches blue pure and simple.
Blue does not exist except as a reaction
between light, air particles and the retina.

That changes the complexion of trees
and means we all paint our own picture.

The pupils colour by numbers
transported in their head from scene to scene.

The reels before them are years long,
but no-one they remotely recognise passes.
If there were no tints or shades
it would seem they were not looking at all,

but lolled about in their swinging chairs,
crooning melodies to help them forget
how little they understood
what shapes connect.

3. Sniff

There are no memories rolling up the streets,
filling the spaces at my hind,
packing themselves into backalley bins,
treasure troves for nozzling.

Nostrils are gun-barrels.
Nothing gets in that isn't for shooting.
Each breeze brings impossible quiz,
no matter how pushed the nerves.

They threaten to discharge
but too much stagnant moisture
has cul-de-sacced the tunnels
and the matter stalls.

Did air ever blow free
through these catacombs,
or was it always snagged by rocky clumps
and made to jump the dam?

4. Taste

The north, south, east and west
of food are all the one.
All the same whether the tongue
flicks, trips, curls or clicks,

there is always a lack.
I find myself full to sick
and I have not tasted
a thick, a lush, a juice or a biting acid.

Buds must have frozen
though it's far from winter.
Sometime I think there were morsels
that turned my tongue

and ran a warm bath in my mouth.
It was a way to live this life.
There could be hope in the swim of juices,
how they are their own medium.

5. Listen

When the vibrations visit
they find the drum flooded
by a sticky sea
of groaning yellow wax.

They can't fly in. They wade
like wellingtoned hunters in rain-sodded fields,
bringing with them the sound of the journey,
as boots do,

and we can't tell what the message is.
There's clamour inside the head
and I find I have lost the thread
of another radio interview.

I am soluble in silence.
There is a sharp fizz
and I am altered.
I remain as a tint, I think.

ALICE

1. Honey

Alice won't stick her hand in the honey jar
and everybody's doin' it doin' it.
Says her fingers will be sticky.
Sticky but golden they say.
Still sticky she replies.
She hates a mess.

She loves the moontaste when it's in,
when she has spooned it past her lips
without a hint of oh-no food
stuck there for all to see.
The river dreams down,
keep your hands inside the car - can't -
and whoosh it's a blast it's living,
down here at the back of the closed mouth.

2. Dinner

Alice took a forkful of carrot he had mashed
and dropped it in her glass of water.
The baby gurgled in his special chair,
the historic walls of the rented terraced house
leaned inwards as if to taunt.
Eamon said nothing.
Alice submerged a piece of potato,
watched the white and orange mingle,
then some mashed cabbage.
This was truer than eating.
Eamon threw down his knife,
let his chair grind before it fell back,
and charged out the door.
That was his way.

WINGS

We sit crushed to the arm-rests of the sofa-bed.
Libra in abeyance.
Last night he came back from a journey
with his arms open
to hug the bosom of the family
and found it flat, the breasts flapping
like tea-towels in the wind.
What had become of it?
I had been sitting at my computer
looking at a past work,
going ape over it,
seeing neither shape nor worth in it.
In the days of his absence
I had brooded over Monday,
how it was always the same.
We had hitched up like two lepers,
poisonous to each other,
fenced against the world.

'She's sulking again',
I hear her say,
as I face the whitewashed wall.

The most important subjects travel far,
from the bottom of the basket,
clambering up through the mountain of fabric,
struggling to the surface
and a glare of censure.

I leave the sweetshop and head for home.
I look for a stone to kick for diversion.

Last Monday:
I have laboured to say this.
You don't know how many hours it has waited
and you take offence.
You mislabel it.
It's not meant to come back here
in that unremarkable brown paper.
It's meant to be touched,
to find its translator,
to be worked upon and modified.
It will wander the sorting offices now
until it finds its proper box
and a messenger's cap.

> *My mother pulls off from the kerb.*
> *She propels herself with three pressings of her foot,*
> *then swings slow and fluid onto the bike.*

I leave the table.
I pretend I'm resigned to your distance.
I'll just have to find myself some company,
come back to you with a concrete plan,
no vague abstractions, roundabout musings
or unthought-out remarks.
You said you don't collect, you travel light.
That's why you treat me like a stranger.
And still you love your family.
You show that with backstrokes and good
providing.
While I, well, tea and no sympathy.

Mammy!

Last Night:
The hum from the road changed
and my stomach went loopy, batty designs,
knots and lopsided twists.
As the key clickered in the lock,
I didn't rush down the stairs,
although doing the opposite
is sometimes doing the same.
When you wanted me to stand embraced,
smiling at the child - a great soap scene -
I pulled away.
You sat beside me and I feverishly typed.
I had cut you out in a rough operation and
my stomach was still twitching.
You might as well have been placenta in a chrome
tray
for all you meant.

> *She doesn't hear me calling.*
> *She'll go home and leave me standing here*
> *on this footpath which is doubling every blink,*
> *becoming Gobi and Sahara*
> *between me and anything.*

You were tired enough to go to bed first.
I did sit-ups and jumps,
tried to shake these knots and loops out.
You seemed to be sleeping when I slid in
backwards, face to the wall.
We lay butterfly bumming
and I planned to wait this one out.
I wasn't moving one more step with you.
No-one lives with an absence.
No-one loves an abyss so deep no echo comes,
after you dragging yourself,
solitary soldier, to the very edge.

If she doesn't stop
I'll die here.
The whole globe
has pulled away from the kerb,
my only ship,
my bed, my floor,
my ground, my gravity,
the only thing that stops
my free fall.

And Tonight
Libra in abeyance on the new sofa-bed,
not so comfortable now it's home.
I'm going to be real here
and if I feel like crying, I will.
It's the Late Late, aftermath of Omagh.
A girl of fifteen has had her lights destroyed,
as if the six stars of blindness had massed together,
each a point on one great disastrous missile
homed on her eyes,
which now drift exploded in a smoking sky.
A woman is angry with everyone
for 'no reason', for this reason -
her son of twelve has left forever with no goodbye.
A woman has lived to marry,
with a plastic transparency on her red raw face,
the inside out of everybody there.

Of course I cry.

Of course you ignore my tears.
But when the choir
goes cacophonous -
maybe it was design -
thirty teenagers and one awful song,
we can allow ourselves a small laugh.

She stops and turns.
I take my place on the carrier
behind her swinging coat
and her slow devoted push.

Would you like some chocolate?
They say it's a good substitute for sex.

GENTLEMAN

Gentleman brought me
two old fish in a new bowl
seven smooth marbles
a satin bag
a t-shirt in green and red
a pair of soft shoes for dancing
ten flavoured sword sheaths
and a Mexican shawl

Gentleman took the plug
out of my mouth
and tasted the wine.
We laughed when we found
it had fine body
let it splutter into a shared goblet
where it stroked the clay
like a lover.

Gentleman pulled
six satin sheets from his pocket
(you'd never think he could, he stood so flat)
and laid me on them like a bouquet.
He took a brush and painted
all the walls a vulvar pink
so everytime I saw them I was cream.

Gentleman chattered
like a bird on coke
while he crushed my buttocks to his groin
made his fingers spider up my solar plexus
said hello to swinging rebels.
He had never felt the like of this
young again as he might wish
the fantasy as lost in dreaming as the dreamer.

SPLIT

On this side of the house I wake to birdsong,
the clockradio blazing all the fours.
Finches and wood-pigeons have no restraint,
twittering on off and during the hour,

you'd think they owned the day.
Look at them, dulcet on the teetering house,
their double-throats giving forth in harmony,
while in here red marks the split.

Red the throat and red the eyes
and red the possibility.
The path of heart is always anginal.
In our room I never heard the birds.

He's on his own these nights in the Mexican bed
and I'm like a country girl in a flat,
sleeping with computers and books, waking
to my notebook and unruffled sheets.

Nothing comes easy but birds at the sun's dial
and my sudden smile when I hear a difference,
a raucous trill among the sweets,
the one who'll always stand alone.

If I had sung more,
I might not have dragged him through this hollow
without a strut or preen, silent as fear,
indexed to the rustle in the brush.

I might have wished him pleasant days
and less in a mutter than I do now,
our faces passing each other like visions
over another uneaten toast and cheese.

THE ORANGE COAT

She got out on a Sunday afternoon,
leaving bubbles to beat Everest in the sink.
Her two teenagers were out loitering
and her husband felling a precarious tree,
all due back by six.

It wasn't hard to pack.
She was brought up on the road,
a servant to impermanence, a snailer.
She knew the necessities and what she could leave,
except for the orange coat.

She placed the note she had written a year before
in a pink envelope on his pine bedside locker,
beside his packet of camels, gold lighter
with his name engraved, an oak's shavings
of bank receipts, bills and pay dockets.

It was cold enough for a winter coat,
October in the moody north of England.
She caught her grey-cushioned eyes and montbretia
hair
in the wardrobe mirror and wished herself dull.
Stretched a desiring hand among the hangers

that veered from its goal and clutched instead
a dark full-length, of unassuming wool.
No need for a dramatic parting scene,
she had broken from that room in little snips
and everything hacked at over time is dead.

She took the battered red van she had bought
with her barmaid's wages, that reminded her
of where she came from, all of England,
her parents people of crafts and strong arms
who would rather die than lodge in bricks and
mortar.

She had thought of them when she bought the
orange coat,
made of cotton, imitation long-haired fur,
a typical gypsy deception, glitter no diamonds,
doesn't matter what's real, it's the feel that counts.
She was a purring tiger in that skin.

'You bring the sun', they'd say to her when she'd
swish
into the pub, orange coat, montbretia hair,
skin loud as a ripe tropical fruit.
It's never enough to shake your lion's mane,
you must turn each pale surface to gold.

Sparks flew from newly laid stones
and drops of water reached for a neutral sky
as she drove day and night towards the west.
She asked for the courage of the bear, its remove
and long claws against those who would trespass in
its cave.

Ended up on an island off the coast of Ireland,
toeing the Atlantic. Hungry, unrepentant sea.
She feeds the birds her dreams of being normal,
on their way to mate, to summer and to nest.
There are more ways than a thousand to tread
earth.

She strolls into a pub, montbretia hair,
five-foot-eight. She can't disguise she's wild.
She's realised, slow learner, it's the woman
makes the weeds. We cast our colours from our
pores,
long and varied. All her threads are from an orange
ball.

ONE SIMPLE THING

He craves one simple thing.
The closest is his mother's smile,
which remains in the fireside chair
she has vacated for the stars.

He's at home in the close fit
of finely-tailored German suits
he still buys in sales,
remembering good times can vanish.

When a project is running as planned,
and other managers fold their arms,
cracking jokes, smiling bland
and bloody-eyed, he smirks and retreats.

He takes the low road to Venus,
beyond the shine of cocktail shakers
and the bath-like comfort of beer,
eschewing the predictable pose

of another graduate in fake fur.
Down the steps to a basement flat
where lights over-rouged are honest
and velvet cushions play confessor.

She waits there, sphinx without malice.
Between her legs a long history
he can read best with his hands.
In the blind unrolling, she makes his skin

a field of poppies, his eyes suns
and his mouth a snapdragon.
She powders his bottom and strokes,
kneads his flesh until he's smooth as glass,

round as a crystal ball.
When he enters the passageway
he looks neither right nor left,
but piles his tribute on the high altar

in a sudden rush and stays to rest upon it,
as if waiting to be sacrificed.
All he has ever wished is to enter the hidden chamber,
to be inside another, if only for a moment.

She closes her legs.
He asks her to open them again and wave as he leaves.
He'll remember her all week
as a smile on a cushioned bed, that simple thing.

ANOTHER GRAFTON STREET

The street shines.
A window's ocean laps you in to ride
among reptilian eyes and bloodless skin.
You're a fish, you say, with satin
pupils, quilted scales and models
holding tightly to your dorsal fin.
There's a limbo dancer, stomachless. You smile.
He's folded backwards, sliding
through your letter-box. Messages, stray things,
you're all-imbibing.
He stops to bow. You believe it's your coin
only that he trades in. You step forward and find
a little sin in his West Indian
polished gleam. He pulls your strings
like floss between his teeth, feelers tense
with loving what is tropical and immense.
You turn your vivid face to mine
and tell me you're a set of petals strung
upon a pair of human legs, a florakin.
Watch, you ask, that you don't fall to bin,
because the dawn is here and you can't stint your
opening.
We buy an ice-cream cone.
You offer it to the sky, a torch to keep the sun
from going supernova in such little time.
4,000 million years, they think,
not enough to lick the cream that sings
in every body on this street,
or hold the hand that takes your note
and offers back some silver.
Nothing is familiar. Chocolate wrappers bring
the history of sun and turn the shop into a fine
museum. Shop assistants morph into Egyptians,

everybody knows some sacred thing,
each word is coded, every crooked smile
a signal from a hidden line,
an army or a band of suitors.
Each yellowed tooth is topical, cousin,
walking Grafton Street with you,
the day you're high.

ALL HER FATHERS

'We've always been close', he once said, 'you and I', and he passed her a brandy. She winced and drank. Drink enough and you can be with anybody. She thinks of the time she went to spend a weekend with a fella in Glasgow and how, when she saw him at the airport, her stomach had turned. Why hadn't it occurred to her to tell him she had changed her mind? In the space of two minutes she had unearthed and buried her disgust. Made up her mind to go through with it, didn't think she had a choice. Only now, fifteen years later, she realises what she could have done. Coward. Gutless. Spent the weekend in a stupor.

She used to puzzle over how men could think they were getting on with her when she could plainly see they weren't. She understands now that presence equals approbation. They were good to her. Mostly what they took was time, and that without malice. They protected her, cosseted her even. She always chose men with high moral standards and then scolded them for their prudishness. 'Always close', her father said, a word she has never associated with him. Stern, domineering, not close.
Selective enforced silence is what she remembers, and what she has got ever after. Either they talk too much or let *her* talk too much, listening in cool, hieratic poses.

But they have laughed too, it must be said, stood and admired when she has lifted her skirt and bent knickerless to the floor, when she has turned

Nirvana on and left her jeans and jumper at their feet. Grateful for a girl who'll give a taste of excitement but never the whole bottle. Doing the daughter, she has been, dancing for her daddy. *My old man keeping away the blues.* Every old man her father. And every young one too. But in her case they inject the blues. They're all controlling, controllable and predictable. Manageable macho men. Safe entities. Men with enough personal problems to make her feel unhappy in a comfortable sort of way.

She becomes the mother they wish they had and the mother often they did have, scolding then mounting them, mocking their accents then sucking them off. She has realised lately, though, now that she looks straight at them and waits to see, that, although their gender have ruled culture, they have put themselves out to please her more than she would for anyone. They've changed their lives for her. They've given her moments when she walked like a queen, when they said her name and brought her gifts wrapped in silver paper so she could pretend she was more than normal. They've made a dream out of her, a myth and a mystic rose, they've kept her skin lifted for months with their kisses and their pretty lies.

One day she'll sit like all the old women and say with a smile that love is an illusion, that men are full of guile. She'll be right but she'll love too the memory of her sons' pretty lies and their careless boisterousness and their one foot over the edge of Moher and their worried look when she said she was tired. She'll envy young girls and understand that without the joys and pains, without that rush

and fight there would be no edge, no falling and, who's to know, no rising. By then her father will be dead and she will have got close, always close, to several men.

SHAPELY

I was born without contrivance
on a day and hour
when the same planets and stars
that watched your mother's lying-in
watched mine, though from different points.
My knees are baked pies,
my nose red at the tip,
my hair straggles like seaweed
and my upperlip is downy
with dark, straight strands.

I have let the hair grow under my arms
and now I can compare them with yours, my darling,
except mine are moss and yours bushes.
I wear like you, dear, clothes for comfort,
but sometimes I play with history,
decking myself with different shapes
so I can recall other lives.

My walk is unschooled
and graceful in that.
I am no baby doll.
My legs swell at the thighs
and their skin quivers like rice pudding
that has soaked in milk for hours
in a homely earthenware pot.
You can neither take me nor make me.
I am not your offspring,
your plaything or your food.
I am the centre of one physical system,
and my own brand of perfect.

A Visit from Odin

Odin called round as a mad-eyed cat,
his head on a stick and its swing like a bird's
speeded up, to this side and back, cinematic.
When he walked it was lightning, a lizard's tongue,
the flit of a desert creature.
He was crouched, as if lintels he knew
were as low as a hand and lower than his eye-
whiskers.
Outside my door with a querulous whine,
his message, as always, in code.

We put down our own cat last week,
with a soundless breath and gaping eyes
green as laurel leaves.
Now his mew laps at the house
and closed windows pine for food.
I thought it was he disturbed the graves
and sent the zombie stalking to our back-door,
but I'd had many dreams of eyes.
Even waking, my hands reached to pull out mine.

So I looked at the Tarot and the tower stared out,
I looked for Horus four times that number
and I met Odin who emptied a socket for song.
Well if it wasn't Odin with a message,
it was the other side of me asking for light.
I want to stare my neighbour in her stony face,
not baulk at the rope and the wall,
nor remain shy at the bottom of the well
like a leaking cup.

Did you know that the schisms are near?
We're drawing our lines in the unset cement.
When it dries it will always be clear where we stand.
The roof will be lifted in the curious hand
of a Giant Child. No-one will hide
in a partitioned office or slouch behind desks.
There will be no closed doors or puckered blinds,
a smile will not pass for social ease,
we will not replace skill with custom.

You'll see grey rabbits then and foxes
and the hounded innocence of the child.
You'll riddle life as a 3-D picture
that waits for your eyes to give it sense.
Focus. As the hidden scene appears
there's always the choice, to dive or turn.
Faith drives you on, steering with no rear-mirror,
never looking back. Keep your eye on the goal
or end up a pillar of salt.

Odin could have failed.
When hanged by the leg from a lone tree
staring into Niflheim's blacks,
he could have cut the rope
and proclaimed premature wisdoms.
His journey would have been small,
the moon captured at the well's end.
Today I stopped looking at the grass
and a thousand daisies popped into my sight
as though I walked across the sky.

AFTER FROST

You took a large knife, dipped it in hot water
and spread icing over the cake.
Then you came back and, with the flat side,
spiked the white until you made a field of frosted
grass.

You know how to do many things you don't value.
You know how to make hot honey with lemons and
cloves,
like the sun in painting mood on the wrangled
hedgerows.
You know how to make frost sound like dried
leaves.

There was a world yesterday that was green and
brown.
Brave flashes of red jumped from the bushes.
We forget it now in this place of frozen growth
where we could be trekking across the land of the
bear.

You can make things clear by taking away crumpled
papers,
washing the walls and giving them a new colour,
so for weeks we are in the nose of new things
beginning to believe we can grasp our lives.

A small hand likes to place itself in the sheath of
your fingers and palm.
The child has every trust that frost and wind will
only hurt

if you deliver him to the artist beyond,
abandoning your own knife, your cloth and your
dripping brush.

Molly's
Daughter

Nuala Ni Chonchuir

Writing is an enjoyable compulsion for me; it excites me. I love the way words work, the way they can be bent and moulded for different voices and moods.

I love to read - my parents gave us the gift of books - and I'm constantly amazed by the work of other writers. I'll read something and wish I'd put those words together in that way. Reading other people's poetry and fiction makes me want to write more and in new ways. My hope is to expose the details of life, both the difficult and the beautiful, using delicate, interesting language. If I can achieve that I'll be happy with my writing.

To Ma and Da
for all the books
and all the love
and to
John, Cúan and Finn
for everything

contents

Note

Some of these poems have been published in *Poetry Ireland Review*, *The Burning Bush*, *The Galway Advertiser*, *ROPES*, *Miscarriage Association Newsletter*, *Books Ireland*, *The Shop*, *Westword*, *West 47*, *Wildeside*, *Electric Acorn*, *Conspire*, *RKS*, *Treasures by the Poets of Ireland* (forthcoming).

MOLLY'S DAUGHTER

Cold next to boney limbs,
the iron bed creaking
beneath a wooden
slatted ceiling.

> *You'll keep your father*
> *away from me,*
> *the last thing I need is*
> *another child to ignore.*

Hair curled around fingers,
then brought next door to
be shown to the visitors
from the city.

> *Isn't*
> *she*
> *only*
> *gorgeous?*

Playing the piano
with a far-away look,
just like Mrs. Darling,
until disturbed by a shout:

> *What's that noise?*
> *Jesus, Mary and Joseph,*
> *will you stop with*
> *that feckin' noise?*

Slip into the kitchen
to watch the men
playing cards
through Woodbine smoke.

Here's a few pence.
Go and buy yourself
some sweets,
like a good girl.

Down to pick flowers
in Darling's field,
slammed against a mossy
bank, dress pulled up.

Just a little feel,
no harm done.
here's a few bob,
don't tell your Mammy.

Back up the lane
to the house,
coins jingling
in a dress pocket.

You're back, are you?
Where did you get
all the money from?
Here I'll mind it for you.

Warm, in your own
room tonight, hearing
the iron bed creaking
with their weight.

Go easy, Joe,
you'll wake her up,
she's not long gone
to bed, you know.

SILVER THIEF

Preening magpie woman,
Eyes ever flicking
To find
The shiniest prize.
A metallic sheen
From your hair.

Hoarding precious trinkets:
Hearts, minds, bodies
Of men.
Your mad clacking
Belies your
Sweet soul.

THE DAY YOU CHOSE TO ARRIVE

for Cúán

You paused just after
your journey began
thinking a retreat might be safer.

But the choice was no longer yours.

> We waited at the rear end
> until, bloody and bruised
> you were hauled out and
> placed on my slackening belly.

Your damp downy head
nuzzled as it should,
while with squinting eyes
you drank your fill.

> A long-limbed stranger
> refueling after the journey.

HEROS, MORPHEUS, HEPHAESTUS

i.m. Seán K.

When you were a novice, the syringe slipping
from your fumbling fingers, did someone tell you
how it went: the liquefying, the angle, the speed?

Or did they grip your arm, pushing their weight
behind the plunge with swift and skilful hands,
their eyes crackling with conspiratorial charm?

Did you ever feel heroic, looking at your mother,
as you hid welts and bruises inside long sleeves
and slipped money from her wallet into your own?

And did you scour the city for the needed signal:
a pair of runners hung like game birds on a wire,
swinging their death knell above empty streets?

Morpheus would have approved - you dared to dream -
but determined to claim you for his own he fused
himself to the firebrand Hephaestus in the end.

Your family around your coffin, their faces in tatters,
wish for the day this day belongs only to memory,
a snowy morning, where the young mourn the young.

THE HAIKU YEAR

Bulbs and buds boasting
new year's arrival:
narcissistic spring.

Cuckoo-spit laden
grassblades, heavy in summer:
frothy larval wombs.

Schools reopening
to hot harvesting weather:
Indian summer.

Silver-white frostwork
sleeping in winter-clad towns:
Yule hibernation.

DUBLIN SON

Borne in the belly of the year, he lay
curled inside, slick as a Liffey salmon
hidden below the bridge by Liberty Hall's
watery windows and oriental rooftop.

He was safely carried, unlike the spewing
youth we glimpsed lying gangle-sprawled
inside a glass phonebox on Eden Quay,
his head lolling as crazily as any infant's.

We vowed to build him the kind of self who
would steer away from the school where
syringes fill the skin and the lessons learnt
are as sinister as Tara Street, empty on Sundays.

Fished out, finally, at leaf-turning time
in a slither of blood and clanging steel,
his first air was drawn from Merrion Square
through belligerent and bellowing lungs.

No longer enclosed under a skin's mound
he swam his course, plotting and planning,
as only he could, the way to go from here,
not too far too soon, was our hope, left behind.

AB INITIO

In the hill-field below the graveyard the cows'
underbellies skim the grass while they deliver
their pats from under slim tails cocked high,
and I avoid their steaming ends and flanks
for fear of being trampled or chewed like cud.

A slitch of trees darkens the side garden which
slopes to the mill race, a no-go place that's
dank with shadow and muck and a crucifix that
lords it over the gloom and Paulus, a gnome,
whom my father blessed with a Latin name.

On the street in front of the houses, paving stones
crosshatch in a neat huddle and the gravel that
slipped into my sandals is gone, if not forgotten,
and the front gardens, where ants would crawl all
summer, are neat and overflowing with tall trees.

But when I go back to these familiar places
where nothing seems to move, I'm left as
sullenly awkward as an unfavoured child, and
it's not the lumbering cattle that cause my fear
but the grip of this place that I no longer call mine.

ANNA'S MEAL

If it had not been for the fighting in Dagestan
the two of us might never have met:
the tinned meat of the Semikarakorsk
processing plant and my digestive system.
I was invited to share a meal with the troops
in a border cellar, two flights down,
and if the darkness wasn't enough to scare,
the slovenly guardian of the kitchen was.

She disembowelled rows of unmarked tins,
slicing the aluminium as easy as silk,
'Tin 23, rotten. Tin 39, the same. Tin 42,
for you. Try a sample of our daily fare,
and tell Moscow how we feast',
and she plunged the blade through each tin,
so I sniffed and licked - what else could I do? -
then spewed my bile all over her floor.

The soldiers earn twenty-two roubles a day,
for no medicine, no fuel, no faith; and for hours
of ducking bullets their bellies are rewarded
with putrid meat from the government's stores.
If it had not been for the fighting in Dagestan
the two of us might never have met:
the tinned meat of the Semikarakorsk
processing plant and my digestive system.

CORK

By Newtwopot House our son mewled
'Are we nearly there yet?'
his soft skin sweltering in the
unseasonal summer heat.
We bounced on through Mallow,
splayed on the edge of black water,
passing meaty roadside patches, the raw
remains of a night-sprinting badger or fox.

On through the marshy city we drove,
a model of southern sophistication,
and out the far side to hills that wore
houses like bright strings of beads.
On twisted roads flanked by cornfields
twenty-five years fell away so that I
became the overheated child wedged
in a waiting game in the back of a car:

While stopped in a lay-by on the
sheep-flanked road to Ballingeary,
I am lifted high to pluck damsons,
their purplish skins blushed with white,
and I roll far-flung names on my tongue:
Timbuktu, Popocatapetl, Kilimanjaro.
These days exotica is reined to places I see:
Gouganebarra, Courtmacsherry, Clonakilty.

LE CAFÉ DE PARIS

Pale and sullen face,
Filling her painted mouth
With Coke,
Cigarette smoke,
Boys' tongues.

Pale and narky face,
Filling her drawn mouth
With pills,
Imagined ills,
Hot gossip.

Pale and bitter face,
Filling her lined mouth
With dread,
Soon be dead,
False teeth.

AFTER THE FUNERAL

Let me recaulk you,
stop the flow,
stay your thoughts.

I will fill the gaping
cracks with saline proof
words - salty sealants.

Though calmness washes over
for a moment, and
nothing drifts through,

like a wind-lashed
vessel, the wet seeps in
and spills out.

Eyes get used to darkness
and learn to see.

POP ART

Geronimo should be hung,
said Warhol, *he's a work of art.*

So he gave him the Marilyn treatment,
and waited for the dollars to roll in.
Which they did.

Get the last of your technicolour
Apache heroes, only ten grand.
And a bargain, at only thirty-seven
more, Mickey Mouse!

Icon after icon in variant colours,
rows of familiar sweet wrappers.
None of them tempting anymore.

Mother

I am the vein
running through
my children,
as they are
pulled from me,
I hold them to me.

I steer a faulty path,
and while avoiding
the potholes and ruts
left in the wake
of my own mother,
I create my own.

I am drawn
to my children,
but as I try
to edge gently
away from them,
they cling to me.

So I scumble along,
making and breaking
rules, until it is
time to winnow
a space with
room only for me.

CONFIRMATION DAY, 1934

Swamped in an overcoat
to hide the long trousers
they got you, instead of
the suit you had prayed for,
you trundled into the church
on worn out feet and sat
alone to wait your turn,
sure that the Holy Spirit would
come down, even to sponsorless boys.

And once the chrism was shining
on your forehead, you slipped
away to trudge the miles
that would lead to the warmth
of an aunt who would feed
you a feast of tea and buns,
and say what a handsome,
holy-looking boy you were.

The sixpence in your pocket was
tightly held all the way down through
The Liberties, but by Islandbridge
your Holy Spirit was flagging; still
you didn't dare ask the Reverend Father
you knew, who squeezed himself
behind the wheel of his car, for a lift
to save your aching feet.

Reaching home by dark,
the voice boomed from the chair:
'How did you get on?'
'Grand', you replied,
wincing as you peeled the heavy
boots from your blistered feet,
and fingering the sixpence
that you had made.

THE WHITE MANTLE

I am Caer, and
when the harvest is over
I seasonally adjust,
slipping through the gap
between this and the otherworld,
where I wear a white mantle
and I rush and slide
on Loch Béal Dragan.

I hiss and glide,
taking comfort in the
throb and thrum of wings
as I fly over Crotta Cliach.
In the hush of the reeds
I slip waist high, then neck deep
into the cooling water, forgetting
my flesh is still feathered.

I invade Aengus' sleep, caressing
his mind - willing him to need
me on waking - I take him
between my thighs and enjoy
the sway of my plump breasts.
He comes, and finds me among
my silver-chained sisters, the only
swan wearing links of gold.

Entwined together, feathers
and arms are made one,
and a shape-changed Aengus
flies three times around the lake
by my side, until we leave for
Brú na Bóinne where our songs
lull the people to sleep, and
my Mac Óg lives only for me.

I am Caer, and I have
discarded my white mantle.

WALSHE'S TERRACE, WOODQUAY

If you could see your house now,
decked in Virgin Mary blue and white,
sunflowers bursting from stainglass,
mosaics trailing a path to the door.
It's a house fit for an angel,
and I can't help thinking that
maybe you live there still, as
a shadow-shape peering from
a corner, wondering at the light
that has washed away the grey.

HUNGER

in Victorian times women affectionately referred
to excess body fat as their 'silken layer'

This body is wrong, so I'll remove
it stone by pound by ounce;
and although I'm not sure
if I'm even here anymore,
I might sometime be thin enough
to be welcomed to their world.

I can peel back this silken layer
with bites not taken, but
I'll never be a companion
to myself, because the bread
I break is in tiny pieces
bartered bites soaked in milk.

I know this is not beauty:
my bones swell, and shadows
creep over my cheeks,
my voice is a rattling hush;
this paper thin skin is a disguise
I wear — I am unsexing for protection.

BLOOD BROTHERS

Apache, Arapaho, Cheyenne,
Comanche, Cree, Crow,
Hopi, Iroquois, Navajo,
Nez Perce, Oglala Sioux,
Pawnee, Shoshone:

these names trip
from my father's tongue -
as lovers of place,
they keep the same faith.

Not forefathers,
but blood brothers.

AFTERNOON TEA

A quarter full, half full, full,

> milk bottles stand in her kitchen,
> brimming with creamy curdles,
> three teabags float in a cup.

Vera sits and tries to make sense of it,

> her dress inside out,
> her cardigan under her dress,
> next doors' flowers in the vase.

Dozens of eggs lie rotting in the press,

> their stink can't help but
> mingle with the milk
> that is standing in bottles

A quarter full, half full, full.

TALAT

The thrum of the gas heater
hovers in the air and
mingles with the prisp of
your kisses on my bared hips.

Your fine arms guide me
along snow-packed pathways
to the hotel bar where our waitress
lumbers like a bear between tables.

We puff on Marlboros,
swapping histories as we laugh,
and you tell me that with a flick of
the wrist what you want is yours.

When you disappear for ten days,
and return nonchalant, I'm as cold
as the light that hangs over
mountain-shadowed Meiringen.

Two refugees: one in exile,
one on a mission of independence.

THIRTY LOST YEARS

for Breda, and her son

Wexford didn't think of me,
when my soul was being bruised
by another woman's indifference.

Leaving by the outer door
I stood numb on Dame Street,
empty armed and only half alive.

The Child of Prague who witnessed
his arrival, lies now at the back of the
wardrobe with those thirty lost years.

But I managed to keep him close to
me by dividing his share, love enough
for seven was spread among six.

SPRING

for Karen

Sitting in your car at Barna pier
we watched the wet light of
evening fall over the Atlantic.

I was sinking under the weight
of my grief, gritting out bitter
words against my family, but

you pardoned my madness, and
I felt less heavy when we headed
for Donnelly's to break bread.

THINGS YOU NEVER SAY

for John D.

I am fishing the air
for assurances,
spinning out a web
where your words
might fall and settle.

But I only have to
read your eyes,
or lie in your arms,
to understand how
deeply you feel.

Thank you for all the
things you never say.

SLOW JOURNEY

My days no longer
have their full sound.

I can't seem to lift my hands
to everyday things,
or settle to ordinary tasks.

Though facing forward,
I'm looking back,
and I can't find the anchor
that will keep me fixed.

Only by tightening
the drifting ropes,
will I be able to make
the slow journey
back to myself.

THE CURRAGH WRENS

We live in the shelter
of the furze, its prickling
plumes our only cover
from the open plain.
No driving rain will
evict us from this place,
not even land-greedy
locals can dislodge us.
We are the oldest of fowl,
and we nestle by those
who need us the most,
loving for a living.

SÍLE NA GIG

My lips splayed
in a hideous grin
pull ecstasy
from my abdomen.
No sweat slides
from my hairline
when my fingers
grapple the folds
resting between
frozen thighs.
These breasts
in relief
feel no caress,
my stoney-eyed
stare warns of
the evils of lust.
I am stone cold,
and left alone.

The Leavetaking

for the O'Connors

Carved from the bones
of only these two,
more of the one
in one or another,
their likeness suffused
and scattered among us,
our legacy a diversity
of form and figure.

They gifted to us
a troublesome honesty,
waspish good humour,
a shy turn of mind,
by gleaning from them
two lifetimes of learning,
we're the possessors of faith
and skills that lie dying.

Home was our sanctuary,
until the downing of tools,
the rooms grew much smaller,
but we were welcome to stay.
The past being history
we took what we could,
and daughter by son
we each drifted away.

The Ideal Drapery

The Ideal Drapery is posted with bills,
the entrance paved with vomit and bins,
the gaping maw of the letter box
leers at young girls in titty tops.

Rats lie trapped in tweedy boltholes
rakishly stacked in dust thick rows,
mannequins pose in moth-chewed frocks,
their wigs askew and their noses lopped.

The smoky masses are belching forth
from Dominick Street's closing doors,
while the ting of the till echoes still,
in anticipation of the ideal customer.

FORGOTTEN HANDS

She has forgotten her hands,
they lie in her lap
curved right under left,
palms exposed to God,
liver spots and ropey veins
temporarily hidden.

      The mice tinkling through
      the piano are old friends,
      photos slip from frames
      so long out of focus
      they hardly bare notice,
      she doesn't mind the damp.

Fingers, thumbs, wrists,
her lined and brittle nails
bear the marks of life,
she holds a firm grasp
to years gone past, her fate
is left in others' hands.

      Dusty lace on the table
      gets lost under a clutter
      of hankies and mints,
      lilac sprigs in a glass
      before Our Lady
      bring comfort in spring.

Struggling to stand she
offers a cheek for a kiss,
talks about the dogs and
all the rest who've left,
short on time, short of breath,
she has forgotten her hands.

BRASS NAILS AND RIGGERS

These lumpen girls, tacked to the footpath
in twos and threes, have fallen away
from hometown ways.

The brass nails in white, spotlessly turned out,
with ear-rings hooped; the riggers are scruff,
less than spruce.

They swagger and call, offering the back lane,
disease, and sweet relief to the desperate
and the young.

At night in a kip on Corporation Street, porter
breath and lipsticked teeth might meet
in a fumbled union.

Country girls, downing a sly jug in the afternoon
in the snug of a welcoming house, small
as a confessional.

MLLE. CLAUDEL

the sculptors Camille Claudel and Auguste Rodin
were lovers for a number of years

I didn't come in the
natural order of things
- infidelity sits well
with my pursuer -
our love is carved
from stone left spare,
while she is the rock
he builds himself on.

I had my own ways
before we two met
- I have long been
angular and jutting -
though others may say
I cleave to his side,
we both know to
whom we belong.

These walls are as
solid as marble
- my hands will lie
idle for thirty years -
but he would swallow
me up, pin me down,
so I have been given
asylum near Avignon.

RAGWORT

Returning home is a falling back in time
to a place where you loom above all,
easily noting the absence of familiars:
the gooseberry and holly bush have been
cleared, to make way for the paired pines
who lord it, where they have no business to be.
But the ragwort remains, with fuchsia and budleia,
filling the air with a wild childhood smell,
that's as clear and understood as the faces
lining the walls of a family reunion.

MAMMY'S LITTLE MAMZER

Mamzer: 'one born of a Prostitute' (Deut. 23:2)

There's little choice for a mamzer
but to follow her Mammy's lead
and make a living from the lewd.

So I ply my trade at crossroads,
a common or garden harlot, gaudy
pendants slung from wattle to waist,
I'm scarlet by name and by nature.
Buyer beware! though I can debauch
as good as any you'll get no divine
intercourse with this wanton wench,
get yourself a sacred whore for that job.
But, my myrrh smeared breasts and
balsam bathed toes - once approached
from the right angle - are guaranteed
to make the most sluggish passion rise.

My Mammy taught me well,
and there being little choice,
I followed her loving lead and
make a living from the lewd.

REQUIEM FOR DINAH

I moulder, no one sees,
I'm the maiden aunt,
the spinster sister whose
genesis will never be.

Her brothers found against
her trysting with Sichem,
so she pleaded to be left
a strumpet, but blades were
whetted, so she'd neither
bear nor rear, though she
was not the one to be cut.

Avenging her despoiling,
with swords and deceit,
they wasted the land of her
pursuer, and left her barren,
condemned an old-maid,
as she bore the guilt of
the slaughter of many.

She wrote her own requiem,
the empty-wombed one,
saying she'd rather have
been branded a whore, and
they prised from her fingers
the skin cut from Sichem,
the only link she retained.

I moulder, no one sees,
I'm the maiden aunt,
the spinster sister whose
genesis will never be.

At A Husband's Funeral

I

I am the Mid-wife,
the penultimate bride you took in this life,
the one for whom L-O-V-E was a decorated fist
flung at the side of my head.

II

Wife One stands silent,
she's the premier leaguer of lovers you left,
the one who took on a simian wreck who quit
her as fast as her youth.

III

Wife Three sobs softly,
saying you'd changed, become a peace loving man,
but we are not moved, the first wife and I,
punchbags, test-wives, fools.

A LAMENT FOR SHORT LIVES

We've put you in the charnel house
along with the bones of the rest,
knowing you'll be in good company;
they'll clear a space for you, maybe
create a form to recognise you by,
and fondly note their own likeness.

For ourselves, we'll stay at the door,
raking through the ashes and silt,
looking for reasons to move on, and
while all the platitudes ever expressed
shroud our minds, one thing is clear:
if this is for the best, it's well disguised.

IN MEMORIAM

Nessa, 1965–2001

We slipped away from you,
left you behind,
shrouded in the white
of another year's winter.
Your slim fingers
crossed on your chest
grasped wilting carnations,
a red bandanna sat snug
on the down that replaced
the jackdaw black mane
that swung down your back.
We joked that the mortuary musak
had hardened your features
and wondered if we'd see
your brown eyes flash at us
from a stranger's face one day,
a small part of you salvaged
and given for good.

Art was your currency:
with oriental intricacy
no lazy eye could prevent,
you mapped out a world in miniature
each detail more perfect than the last;
and you who envied the articulate
were always more fluent than most.

On the postcard you sent
from your last great adventure
- a pilgrimage to Lourdes -
you proclaimed it 'a tackfest':
'Blackpool meets the Vatican', you wrote,
your head wrecked with your
fellow pilgrims' strident religiosity.

I wish I could pluck the sounds
of our last conversation from the air
and savour each word, each syllable:
your hope, maybe, and my sorrow.
I want to tell you now
that my baby boy is born,
that your red-haired girl
loves her food, just like us,
that she orders people around,
just like us, and that she is given
love enough for ten little girls.

When you slipped away,
stayed behind in that old year,
who went with you?
Did you think about us?
While we remain here
all that's left for us to do
is to close our eyes and
let the memory of you
act as salve to our wound.

MOVING WEST

Darkness seeps slow,
draws back the glow from the east,
covers this raintown in a blanket of grey,
hangs a fingernail moon to draw the eye up
through a lattice of trees emptied of green,
claws its way back to the ground.

I find myself here,
so I name it my home and settle for that,
accepting the wary welcome when offered,
likewise the deluge that roils its way down
through the saltwatered air on the streets,
flushing this seatown of light.

TRINITY

Three telegraph poles scale the hill
and stand like the crosses at Calvary,
admiring the rain sodden landscape,
the russets and plums of November.

We turn the car at Peacocke's Cross
to catfight our way past lapping water,
on this penitent late-Sunday drive we're
one pair blood-tied, the other mated.

We move through the Maam Valley,
made silent by its bleak majesty,
secure against unending squalls,
our familiar and fractious Trinity.

OLYMPIA

Poached from the company
of her late evening wine,
and coaxed into posing,
she wears nothing but assurance,
her slight body a river of curves.

Perched against pillows
she possesses the attention,
and invites coy caresses,
she reigns only on canvas,
her skin bearing a faultless sheen.

Swallowed up in a bottle
she hawks paintings to drunkards,
takes ladies for lovers,
and is christened 'La Glu',
her full-toned form now fading.

Soon-Ae's Lament

At thirteen, why did I have to know
the push and heave of so many men,
unleashing war-woundings on me,
their sweaty skin slick on mine?

Tagged 'essential military supplies'
in logbooks with saki and guns,
cargoes of girls shipped from home,
to bring comfort to men being men.

I was kept, waiting in pain, for the
line at my door to dwindle and die;
laid in my room the comforts of comfort
women: a pallet, a mattress and lies.

Soldiers awarded time on a ticket,
crush and rape as relief from war,
'Emperor's orders', they say to explain,
drawing blood from girls locked in fear.

My scars are all over, within and without,
and I whisper now to be heard: I'm lonely,
can't walk well, I want someone to say sorry
to this ghost crawling her way through life.

LIVESTOCK

The Freshwater Bay banbhs
skirt the sow's ankles
puddling in the muck.

Their cloven-hooves blister
under lightening bellies
and downturned eyes.

The slaughterhouse keeper
at the Cheale abattoir
remarks on their limping.

Their cocked tails question
this lameness and dribbling:
foot-and-mouth disease.

THE MODEL

She was swallowed up
by the pea-green Seine,
its murk lapped over her,
pulling her into its belly,
a sorrow-drowned nap
underneath the Pont Neuf
ending with a watery slip
into the reeking roils.

In life she longed to pose,
to be frozen in paint,
garbed as a young boy or
maybe an unchaste Diana,
and though plain as milk,
she paced the place Pigalle
to be passed over for more
pinched or rollicking types.

Slabbed in the morgue,
she is sketched from life,
a cadaver in some canvas,
a cheap anatomy lesson,
who will rot on the pages,
like in the paupers' grave,
where she'll lie with the rest
of the forgotten of Paris.

NIGHT RAT KILLERS

The Daily Telegraph, 18 October 1993

Scattering through Bombay's side streets
the barefoot killers swing clubs and torches,
a clutch of stenches swarms around them,
and punctured skin pockmarks their arms.

Risking sixty-odd diseases, they bag rats
as big as cats for fifty five rupees a night,
not enough to live on, but enough to buy
some dahl, cheroots and an occasional Coke.

SCRIMSHAW

Before we reach final landfall
this piece will be scrimmed:
a tooth plucked from the maw
of a heaving sperm whale,
his molar more precious to me
than his head's oily milk.

I have bathed it in brine,
rubbed the ivory curve with
a shark-skin slitch,
buffed its butter-yellow length
until it's ready to receive
a veil of etchings and India ink.

With the smallest of jacknives
I whittle the lines,
carving at time,
and *The Susan* bucks under me,
greedy as a Nantucket hussy
pinioned by a sailor's weight.

I don't make corset busks,
jagging wheels or yarn swifts,
but carve the likeness of the one
who craves for me at home,
her arched belly as plump
as a mainsail full with wind.

But as months roll into years
and whalesong makes me weary,
I chase her face to capture it down,
and wonder if my offerings
can be enough: a pouch of dollars
and this piece of scrimshaw.

EEL

To push him towards death,
he is placed in a cross
that we have scratched
into the dirt of the riverbank,
with air puffed gill-slits,
he gathers a coating of dust,
and sloughs off life like a skin.

He's no slick-bodied elver:
the dark back and silver belly
- his cover in the brackish Liffey -
show it's years since he lumbered
from the Sargasso Sea,
a gauzy glass-fish scudding
through time and waves.

Death comes to him slowly,
so we bludgeon his head and
coil his smooth-ribbon length
into a canvas bag,
but once flayed, sliced and fried,
I refuse my share,
wary of his unholy crucifixion.

I prefer prey who cannot
scatter though grass,
the small and inedible
that can be slipped back into
mud and riverwrack:
minnow, roach, frogspawn,
a less knowing type of breed.

ANILINE

Arsenical Schweinfurt Green,
dressed many a fine lady's skin,
then seeped in deadly waves from walls
to poison the children of the poor.

But when the lady's lips became scabby
the dyeworks was forced to close
and the owner was made to carry
fresh water to the richman's door.

Not to the poorman's, you understand.

KNOCK

Ox-eye daisies peep from ditches
as we sweep north
on our summer pilgrimage,
the family holiday finally begun.
I beg to stop at Knock,
attracted by the kitsch-fest glimpsed
through the high-season drizzle
in the shops that line the footpath.

Safe inside from the rain,
a red-robed Jesus lords it over
a gaggle of plaster saints who crowd
around the Mother Teresa water font
and a framed now-you-see-Her,
now-you-don't Virgin apparition.
I finger Padre Pio paperweights
and Our Lady of Knock sticks of rock
that are packed with more e-numbers
than could be safe at one sitting.

Twirling a stand of rosaries,
their beads a festival
of crystal, marble, wood,
I listen to the shop assistants
compare hangovers
and name off the pubs
they crawled between last night,
all the while hawking
their shiny gew-gaws
to the eager holy hordes.

AND WHAT DID WE SEE?

a raft of dol-die-dees
lining the streets of Knock:
hollow Virgins, outsized rosaries
and Bakelite saints,
gaudy enough for any
Poundshop

a Táin's worth of black bulls
lumbering across a hill
near Gartan Bridge
their horns glinting like crescent moons
through the drizzle
shortly after we crashed the car

a tangle of boats
skewed along the harbour
in Killybegs
and the combed flank of Ben Bulben
hunched above Sligo town
and Yeats cold in his grave

AT THOOR BALLYLEE

It has the same fusty smell
of every Irish tourist attraction,
and a collection of dusty artefacts
displayed against walls slick with damp
and interpreted by Abbey-voiced men.

But the 'old millboards and sea-green slates'
planted by the peaty wash of the Cloone
hold a power that even the gift shop's
neon Yeats yo-yos can't take away,
despite the poet's wishes for simplicity.

As we leave the cold turret stairs
for the battlements and the welcome fug
of our Indian summer I, being a mother,
hope that the glow from local turf
kept their children warm and well.

Someday from our own retreat
- a cottage, fields full of cow-dung -
our children will enjoy
the same bird's sleepy cry
among the deepening shades.

LIFFEY

for Ma and Da

Reaching out from Wicklow's peat hags
and stretching into Poulaphouca,
she is home to eels, kingfishers
and the white bones of the dead.

Stacked one behind the other
bridges grip her arm like bracelets
and her veins are the tea-brown spill
of the Tolka, the Poddle and the Wad.

Boats chase the length of her wrist
and plunge on past the Muglin Rocks,
pushing a path through mud and fish,
pointing their way out to sea.

BRIDGET F. - INMATE - GALWAY GAOL

for Geraldine C.

1880
I was hungry so
I set traps at dusk
for the hares that lie
in shallow beds
around the Corrib.
I caught one,
sliced her pale belly
and out plopped
a sack of leverets,
small and slippy;
the magistrate asked
if I'd enjoyed my meal.

1883
In the courtroom
they said that I had
a bad character
- called me a
girl of ill-fame -
they put my palms
across my chest
like a corpse
and took a picture,
the photographer said
that my forty-four years
hung heavy on me.

1885

The gaoler called me
a strumpet and took away
my bonnet and shawl,
I unteased ropes
until my fingers bled
and thought of sailors
I had once known,
and the small drop
that warms the gut;
in the evenings they
fed us on buttermilk,
potatoes and beef.

MARY W.

Mary, a Galway thief, was nearly blind

Grangegorman Prison

They have sent me east,
more than a hundred miles,
to a place with hard air
and no fishy smell of the sea.

I'm here for the sake
of pockets picked in Castlebar
that only got me a few
pawn tickets and a miser's purse.

Now who will show me
where to step when my head rages
and my eyes black out,
who will warm me at night?

Goldenbridge Refuge

I have been shipped
across the murky Liffey
to a place even worse than the last
for hucksters and mad women.

I bite my skin, make my hair wild,
and roll my one good eye,
I even say that I'll burn every
whore of them in their beds.

I want them to send me back
because how will my man
know where I am
when I can't even see for myself?